ÉCOLE NORMALE SUPÉRIEURE DE FONTENAY-SAINT-CLOUD

CRÉDIF

CENTRE DE RECHERCHE ET D'ÉTUDE POUR LA DIFFUSION DU FRANÇAIS

# Les petits lascars

# LE GRAND LIVRE DES HISTOIRES 2

MICHÈLE GARABÉDIAN • MAGDELEINE LERASLE • FRANÇOISE PÉTREAULT-VAILLEAU

Dessins de Anne Bozellec

crédif

Maman
va au marché

Aujourd'hui, c'est le marché.

« Hum, ça sent bon ! »

« Oh là là ! Comme elles sont grosses ! »

Maman achète des légumes.

«Voilà Madame... les radis et le chou-fleur.»

«Tiens, Céline!
Où est Céline?
Céline?»

Maman cherche Céline. Elle va à gauche, elle va à droite.

«Céline!                    Céline!»

4

Voilà Céline devant les fleurs...

« Ah ! Te voilà ! Ouf ! »

« Tu ne dois pas partir toute seule !
Tu vas te perdre ! Le marché est grand... »

Maman n'est pas contente...

« Maman, je veux des fleurs pour Mamie.
Comme elles sont belles ! Et elles sentent bon ! »

Quelle peur ! Maman et
Céline rentrent à la maison.

5

# Céline à l'école

Céline arrive à l'école. Elle retrouve ses camarades.

« Bonjour Maîtresse ! »          « Bonjour Céline ! »

Elle va dans le coin cuisine.
Les enfants font la vaisselle.
Céline lave une assiette avec l'éponge,
puis une fourchette, un couteau,
et un verre en plastique.

Les enfants vont dans la salle de jeux en chantant.

Ils jouent.

« Venez, nous allons danser ! »

Ils vont aux toilettes.

9

Maintenant les enfants travaillent.
Céline dessine un bonhomme avec sa copine.

C'est la récréation.
« Nous allons  sortir. »

« Tu te trompes ! »
« Mais non ! C'est comme ça. »

Les enfants s'amusent.

« Attrapez-moi ! »

Les enfants retournent dans la classe.

Sur le tapis, ils chantent *Une Souris verte*.
La maîtresse raconte une histoire.

Céline va à l'atelier peinture :
elle peint une grosse souris.

C'est bientôt l'heure des mamans,
les enfants prennent un livre à la bibliothèque
et ils attendent.

«Tu mets du vert?»

«Non,
je mets du jaune.»

« C'est midi !
Prenez vos manteaux ! »

« Au revoir Céline ! À cet après-midi,
tu feras la sieste. »

« Au revoir,
Maîtresse ! »

« Oh ! Une tête de maman. Encore une ! »

L'aspirateur

« Nous sortons avec Céline.
Vous avez bien compris,
Olivier et François :
vous rangez et vous nettoyez
la chambre. »

« Oui Maman, au revoir. »
« Je prends l'aspirateur. »
« Voilà Vroum-vroum-
super-gros-bruit
qui se bat
avec la poussière. »

« Tu ranges les jouets
et les livres,
moi je passe
l'aspirateur. »

« Non, moi, je passe
l'aspirateur. »

« Non, c'est moi
parce que je suis plus grand. »

« Bon d'accord. »

«C'est presque fini, je passe sous le lit...»

Vroum, vroum...

«Oh qu'est-ce que c'est?

Hop, c'est parti dans l'aspirateur!»

«C'est quoi?»

«C'est comme un petit mouchoir
bleu et blanc avec un nœud»     «C'était où?»     «Sous le lit de Céline...»

«C'est son câlin-dodo,
elle le prend pour s'endormir...»

17

« Voilà Maman ! »

« L'aspirateur a avalé le câlin-dodo de Céline.
Qu'est-ce qu'on peut faire ? »

« Prenons l'aspirateur. »

« Maman, viens vite ! »

« Nous allons regarder
à l'intérieur de l'aspirateur
dans le sac à poussière. »

« Tu ouvres
le ventre de l'aspirateur ! »

« Mon câlin-dodo,
mon câlin-dodo ! »

« Pauvre Vroum-vroum !
Il a mal ? »

« Et voilà le câlin-dodo de Céline. »

« Bravo Maman ! »

« Ah, mon câlin-dodo ! Il est tout sale ! »

« Je vais le laver. »

« Pardon Maman,
demain François
passera l'aspirateur :
il est petit mais
il voit bien par terre. »

« Oh oui, je suis le meilleur
conducteur d'aspirateur.
Regardez. »

« Vroum-vroum !
Oh oui,
tu es un bon chauffeur ! »

19

Olivier
sous la pluie

Olivier sort de l'école. Il rentre chez lui.
Oh! Qu'est-ce que c'est?
Une goutte de pluie...

Flic, floc, flac, c'est la pluie.
Olivier met
sa capuche.

Flic, floc, flac, la pluie tombe sur lui. Est-ce qu'il est mouillé?
Non, parce qu'il a son ciré jaune et ses bottes en caoutchouc.

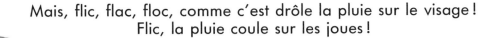

Mais, flic, flac, floc, comme c'est drôle la pluie sur le visage !
Flic, la pluie coule sur les joues !

Flac, une goutte lui chatouille le nez !

Floc, la pluie mouille ses cheveux !

Floc, une goutte lui tombe
sur le bout de la langue !

Olivier ne regarde pas par terre et... floc ! Qu'est-ce que c'est ?
Olivier a mis le pied dans une flaque... Une grosse flaque d'eau !

Clap, clop, Olivier tape des pieds et l'eau saute.
Olivier tape plus fort : clip, clap, clop, clap, clip, clop !

Mais il pleut de plus en plus fort.
Vite, vite, Olivier court à la maison.
Dans la maison, il ne pleut pas !

Ouf, il est à l'abri !
Oh... Que se passe-t-il ?
Il y a de l'eau dans ses bottes ;
et c'est très froid.

François
est malade

Ce matin, François est dans son lit;
il est malade...

Maman téléphone au docteur.
«Allô! Mon fils est malade,
Il a très mal à la tête...
Vous pouvez venir?»

«Oui, je viens tout de suite,
je cours, je vole.»

Le docteur arrive.
François est couché dans son lit,
il a la tête toute rouge
comme une tomate.

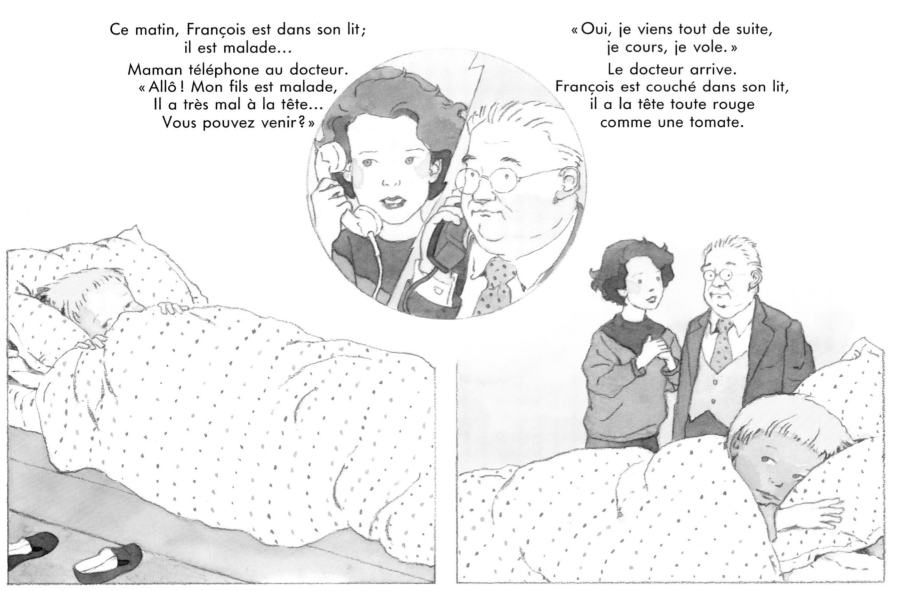

25

«Est-ce qu'il a de la fièvre?»
«Oh oui, 38°.»

Le docteur ausculte François.

«Est-ce que tu tousses?»
«Oui, je tousse.»

«Est-ce que tu te mouches?»

«Non, je ne me mouche pas.»

«Est-ce que tu as mal à la tête?»

«Oui, j'ai mal à la tête.»

« Est-ce que tu as mal au ventre ? »

« Non, je n'ai pas mal au ventre. »

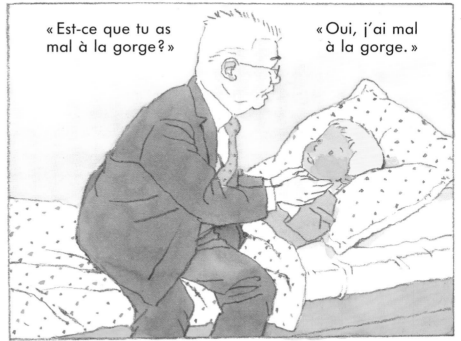

« Est-ce que tu as mal à la gorge ? »

« Oui, j'ai mal à la gorge. »

« Montre-moi ta gorge et dis aaah… »

« Aaah… »

«C'est une angine, Madame. François, tu vas rester à la maison pendant huit jours ;
tu prendras bien tes médicaments. » «Oui. »

«Alors, trois comprimés par jour
et trois cuillères de sirop,
un peu d'aspirine.
Au revoir François, repose-toi bien
et reste au lit. »

«Au revoir docteur, je vais guérir ? »

«Mais bien sûr
et tu raconteras ta maladie à l'école ! »

28

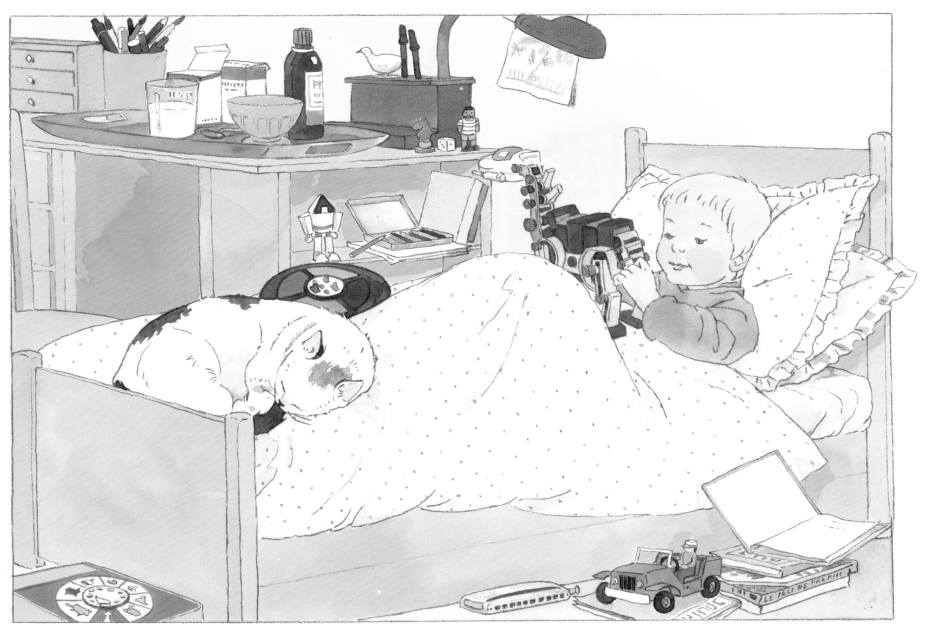

# Le bain de Céline

« Céline, Céline, le bain est prêt ! »

Céline va dans la salle de bain.
Elle se déshabille :
pull, pantalon, chaussettes…
et hop ! dans la baignoire.

Maman prend un gant de toilette
et frotte le savon.
« Hum ! Que le savon sent bon ! »

«Céline, ne bouge pas! Ne tape pas des pieds!»

Maman lave tout le corps de Céline,
le ventre, les jambes, les pieds...

«Céline, assieds-toi pour rincer le savon.»

«Je lave maintenant les bras,
sous les bras, le cou,
attention, le visage!»

«Aïe, aïe, ça pique les yeux!»

«Eh bien, ferme tes yeux, n'agite pas tes pieds, tu mouilles ma robe.»

«Aïe, aïe, le savon pique les yeux!
Je pleure!»

Olivier entre.
« Pourquoi tu pleures ? »

« Elle a du savon dans les yeux,
elle bouge sans arrêt... »

« Allez, pleure plus...
Regarde ce que je vais faire
avec le savon. »

Olivier fait une grosse bulle,
puis une autre, c'est beau !

« Oui, c'est beau. Encore une fois, fais encore une bulle ! »

33

« Non, tu sors Céline.
Olivier, donne-moi la serviette. »

« Brrr...
j'ai froid. »

« Aide-moi Olivier,
frottons bien fort la pauvre petite Céline
puisqu'elle a froid !!! »

« Hi, hi, hi,
vous me chatouillez !
Maintenant j'ai chaud. »

« Bon, un coup de brosse, et hop !
Enfile ton pyjama pour la nuit. »

# L'anniversaire de François

Aujourd'hui c'est l'anniversaire de François : il a six ans.

« Vite, François, ouvre la porte !
Voilà tes petits camarades. »

« Bonjour ! Bonjour ! Bonjour les enfants ! »

Tous les petits copains de l'école sont là...
Sébastien, Danièle, Brahim, Baptiste et Noémie.

Les enfants portent de gros paquets de toutes les couleurs.

« Il faut ouvrir les paquets ? »

François prend le paquet de Sébastien, Danièle et Brahim.
Il coupe le ruban et enlève le papier.

« Oh, une voiture de pompier...
Elle est toute rouge ! »

Voici le cadeau de Baptiste et Noémie.

« Et tu as vu l'échelle :
comme elle brille ! »

« Waou ! Le robot ! »

« Avec le casque
et le bouclier ! »

«Et notre paquet, tu l'ouvres?»

François ouvre le paquet de Céline et Olivier, il enlève un papier, puis un autre, encore un autre...

Mais où est le cadeau?
Oh! Une petite balle...

Tous les enfants rient...

« C'est une farce !
Tiens voilà ton cadeau… »

« Oh, un piano…
Merci, merci,
vous êtes tous gentils ! »

« Maintenant ! À table ! »

Sur la table il y a des assiettes,
beaucoup de friandises jaunes,
rouges et des bouteilles.

« Asseyez-vous ! »

40

La lumière s'éteint : Madame Lascar apporte le gâteau.
« Attention François ! Il faut souffler les bougies… »
« Un, deux, trois. » Pfff…
« Bravo ! Joyeux anniversaire ! »

# Le carnaval à l'école

«Maman, c'est aujourd'hui le carnaval?»

«Oui, ton costume est prêt,
viens dans la salle de bain.»

François a un pantalon noir et un pull noir.
Maman découpe un morceau de tissu
et le met sur la tête de François.

«Regarde-moi Céline...
Je suis quoi?»

«Je ne sais pas...»

43

Maman prend un crayon :
elle dessine un trait autour des yeux
et des moustaches autour de la bouche.
Elle colorie le bout du nez de François en rose.

« Miaou, miaou !
Grr... Grr... ! »

« Un chat !
Tu es un chat ! »

« À moi Maman ! À moi ! »

« Et sur le visage ! »

Maman habille Céline :
un pantalon à rayures blanches et noires,
une chemise verte
et un gilet à carreaux verts et rouges.

«Je passe de la crème blanche sur le visage.
Je fais des traits autour des yeux.
Je mets du rouge sur les lèvres et sur le bout du nez.»

«Je mets mon chapeau. Je suis qui?»

«Un clown!»

«Maintenant,
en route pour l'école!»

Dans la cour de l'école,
il y a beaucoup d'enfants déguisés.

« Regarde ! Un boxeur...
et là-bas une infirmière ! »

« Oh ! Un canard tout jaune !
Et la sorcière, brrr...
elle n'est pas belle... »

Tous les enfants rient,
ils se disent bonjour et ils font des rondes.
« Allez viens Céline ! Nous faisons une farandole.
Prends ma main ! »

La farandole est de toutes les couleurs... bleue, verte, noire, blanche, rose, jaune, marron...
La farandole a des rayures, des carreaux, des ronds, des fleurs...

«Demain c'est Carnaval?»

Maintenant c'est l'heure du goûter.
Les enfants rentrent à la cantine.
Les enfants mangent des crêpes.

«Ah non, pas tous les jours!»

Céline prend le train
avec Mamie

Céline prend le train avec Mamie.
Elles vont à Lyon.

« Allez vite, montez. »

Maman embrasse
Mamie et Céline.
« Assieds-toi à
côté de la fenêtre. »

51

On entend un coup de sifflet, le train démarre.

«On roule
doucement Mamie!»
«Attends! Nous allons
rouler très vite après!»

Céline             regarde les maisons, les voitures par la fenêtre.

52

Maintenant le train roule très vite.
Céline écrase son nez sur la vitre.

«Mamie, je ne peux pas bien regarder
les champs et les maisons.
Nous allons vite !»

«Mamie, pourquoi ça s'allume
au-dessus de la porte là-bas?»

«Cela signifie qu'une personne est dans les W.C.»

«Céline, Céline réveille-toi, voilà Lyon!»

«Oui, elle nous attend, viens vite!»

Le train s'arrête...
Mamie se lève et s'habille.
Tout-à-coup, quelqu'un
frappe à la fenêtre.
«Oh Mamie!
Voilà Tante Catherine!»

# L'histoire de Blanchette

Les trois enfants sont dans le salon. Papa raconte une histoire.

« Dans le Jura, il... »

« C'est quoi le Jura ? »

« C'est une région de France. »

« Je vais vous raconter l'histoire
d'une petite vache qui s'appelle Blanchette.

Elle est blanche et marron ;
elle a de grands yeux marron et deux petites cornes ;
elle porte autour du cou une grosse cloche. »

«Tous les soirs, Blanchette et ses amies
vont dans le pré pour manger et dormir.»

«Elles dorment dehors?»

«Oui, les vaches dorment dans les prés.»

« Sur le chemin, on entend le bruit des cloches :
ding, ding, ding. Toutes les vaches sont
joyeuses d'entendre le bruit de leurs cloches. »

« Un soir, toutes les vaches sont dans le pré.
Elles sont tranquilles. »

«Tout à coup, une grande ombre passe entre les vaches.

L'ombre s'approche de Blanchette et zipp !... lui arrache sa cloche. »

«Oh ! Pauvre Blanchette. »

« Aussitôt Blanchette crie : «Meuh, meuh! Au voleur, au voleur!
Meuh, meuh! Ma cloche!»
Toutes les vaches courent à gauche, à droite;
toutes les vaches courent dans le pré.
«Meuh, meuh, le voleur est là!» crie une vache.
Blanchette fonce sur le voleur, cornes en avant.»

« Ah, bravo Blanchette ! »

«Alors, le voleur prend peur et lâche la cloche. Il saute par-dessus
la barrière et il court, il court...
Ding, ding, toutes les vaches font sonner leur cloche.
Blanchette a retrouvé sa cloche. Meuh, meuh... Les vaches font la fête.»

Papa ferme le livre et les enfants vont dormir.

Couverture : Hans Troxler

 Aubin Imprimeur, 86240 Ligugé. — D.L. avril 1991. — Impr. P 37458

# our big table

# Our Big Table
### What We Eat and Where It Comes From

Originally published as:
**miam la nature**
Comment poussent les frites et la pizza

Text, illustrations and layout:
© Lisa Voisard · www.lisavoisard.ch

Translation from French: Jeffrey K. Butt
Typesetting: Ewelina Proczko
Editor: Angela Wade
Proofreader: Karin Waldhauser

ISBN: 978-3-03964-065-2
First edition: April 2025
Deposit copy in Switzerland: April 2025
Printed in China

HELVETIQ publishing is being supported by the Swiss Federal
Office of Culture with a structural grant for the years 2021–2025.

helvetiq.com

Lisa Voisard

# our big
# table

## What We Eat
## and Where It Comes From

Translated from French by
Jeffrey K. Butt

# Table of Contents

Is your tummy rumbling? If so, it means you're hungry! Food gives us energy and that's why we have to eat every day. In other words, eating is a basic need. But it's also a time to share and have fun! Certain flavors can sweep us away to exotic places, while others can be comforting or trigger a memory.

But before you bite into that apple, have you ever thought about where it comes from? Have you ever seen broccoli growing in a vegetable garden? How does a bitter cacao bean become a delicious piece of chocolate? And who invented popcorn?

Let your curiosity run wild! It's so important to know where our food comes from.

We're so lucky to live on a planet with such an abundance of tastes and colors. So, let's pay a little more attention to it, our bodies and the food we eat!

# Pull up a chair!

Whether it's for a family get-together, a birthday party or just dinner, sitting around the table and sharing a delicious meal brings us closer!

# Grow, little plant, grow!

Much of what we eat comes from the ground. There is no bread without first harvesting wheat. To get chocolate, a cacao tree has to grow. And if we want jam, we have to pick berries. It's a good thing there are so many different types of plants, because we need variety in our diet!

## Water

Roots absorb water and nutrients from the soil. Then, sap carries them to the leaves and flowers.

## Soil and space

To grow roots and get food, plants need rich, healthy soil. And to grow properly, they also need plenty of space.

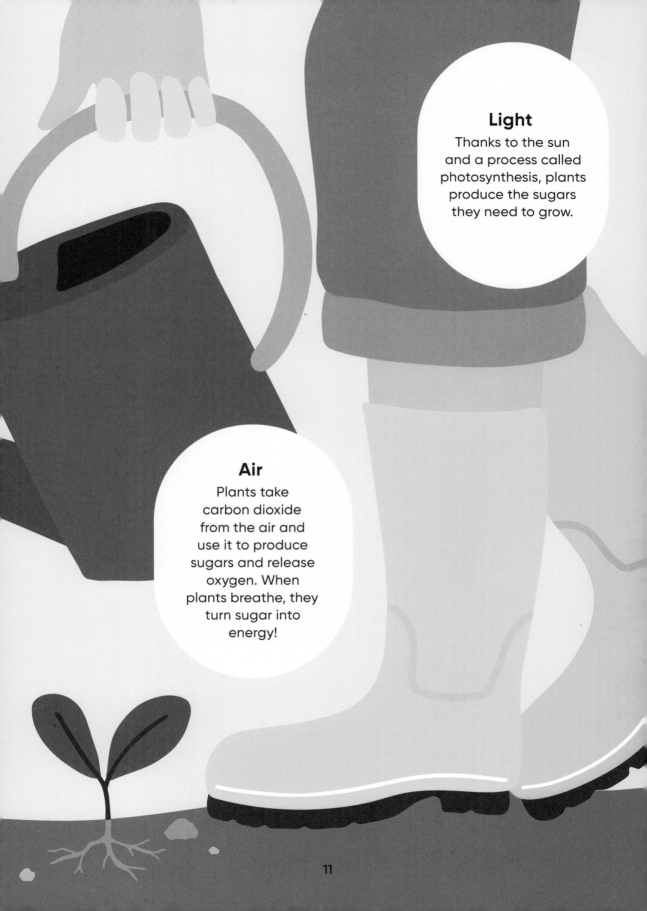

**Light**
Thanks to the sun and a process called photosynthesis, plants produce the sugars they need to grow.

**Air**
Plants take carbon dioxide from the air and use it to produce sugars and release oxygen. When plants breathe, they turn sugar into energy!

# How do they grow?

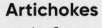

## Artichokes

We eat the flower of the plant. It grows on top of a long stalk that can be over three feet tall!

## Pineapples

Before being cut for market, pineapples grow on a tall stem surrounded by leaves.

## Brussels sprouts

We eat the buds that grow in tight bunches along the stalk.

## Kiwis

Kiwis grow on very long vines, where they dangle on stems.

## Peanuts

Peanut plants are 20–90 cm/8–35 inches tall and their fruit grows in pods in the ground. Each pod usually holds two seeds: the peanuts we eat!

## Broccoli

The part of the broccoli plant we eat is a mass of tightly packed flowers known as an inflorescence.

**Brussels sprouts** have a strong smell and can be bitter.

**Lettuce** can have a funny texture.

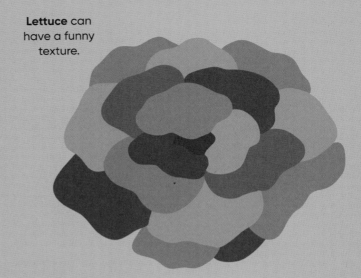

Sometimes, **spinach** doesn't look very appetizing.

# Yuck, this is gross!

Some people just can't stomach food that has a strange taste or texture.

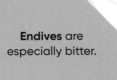

**Endives** are especially bitter.

To some, **cilantro** (or **coriander**) tastes like soap. It's a genetic thing that varies from person to person.

Yummy, melt-in-your-mouth **chocolate** stimulates the pleasure hormone!

**Carrots** are sweet and there's no veggie children love more!

# Yum, this is gooood!

It's easy to love foods that have lots of sugar, salt and fat . . . they activate pleasure hormones in our brain!

Juicy and sweet, **strawberries** are simply delicious.

**Ice cream** is an irresistible marriage of cold and sweet!

The fat and salt in **French fries** make them hard to resist!

## Taste and color
What foods do you like and dislike? Do you know why?

# Bananas

Every supermarket sells this long yellow fruit that gets little brown spots when it's overripe. While it's grown almost exclusively in the Southern Hemisphere, the banana is one of the most commonly exported and eaten fruits in the world.

Bananas grow in bunches called . . . bunches!

Flower

Banana trees are not trees. They're actually herbaceous plants, like palm trees, and that's because they don't produce wood.

"Banana" comes from the Arabic word *banan*, meaning 'finger.' When several bananas are joined together, we call them a 'hand.'

## What's the right way to peel a banana?

Usually, we peel bananas from the top, by pulling on the stem. But it's actually more practical to do as the monkeys do and peel from the bottom!

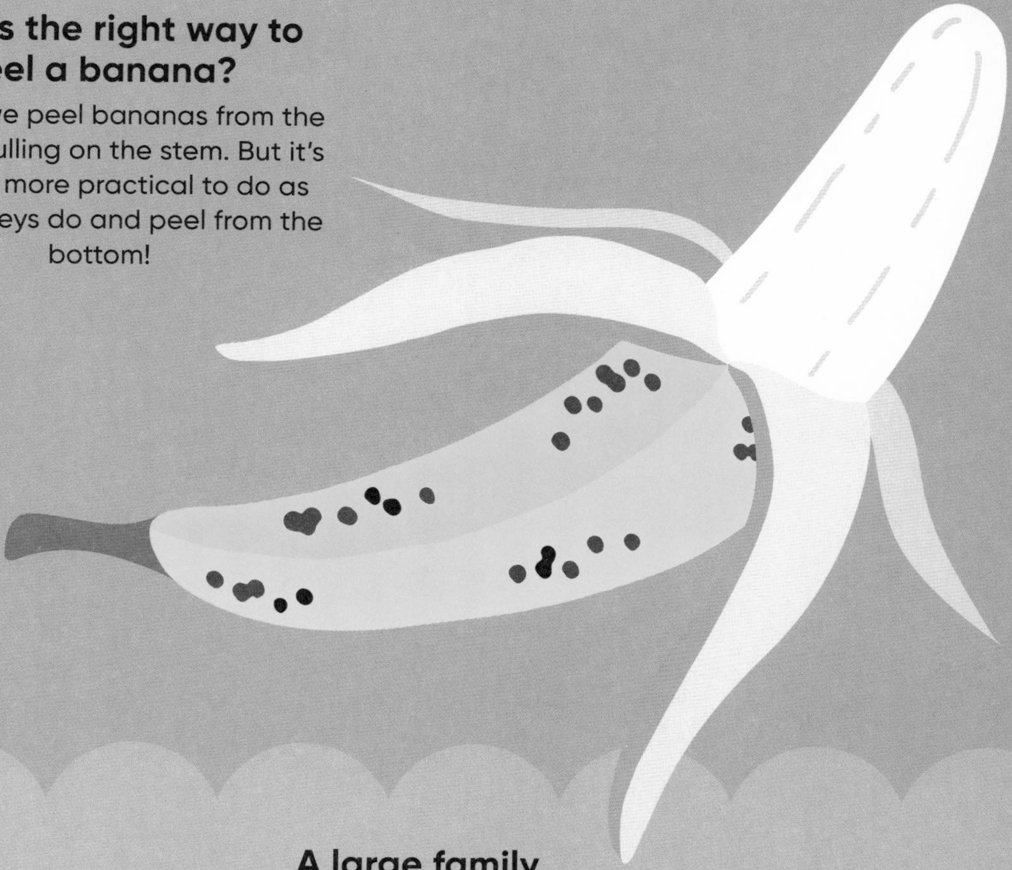

## A large family

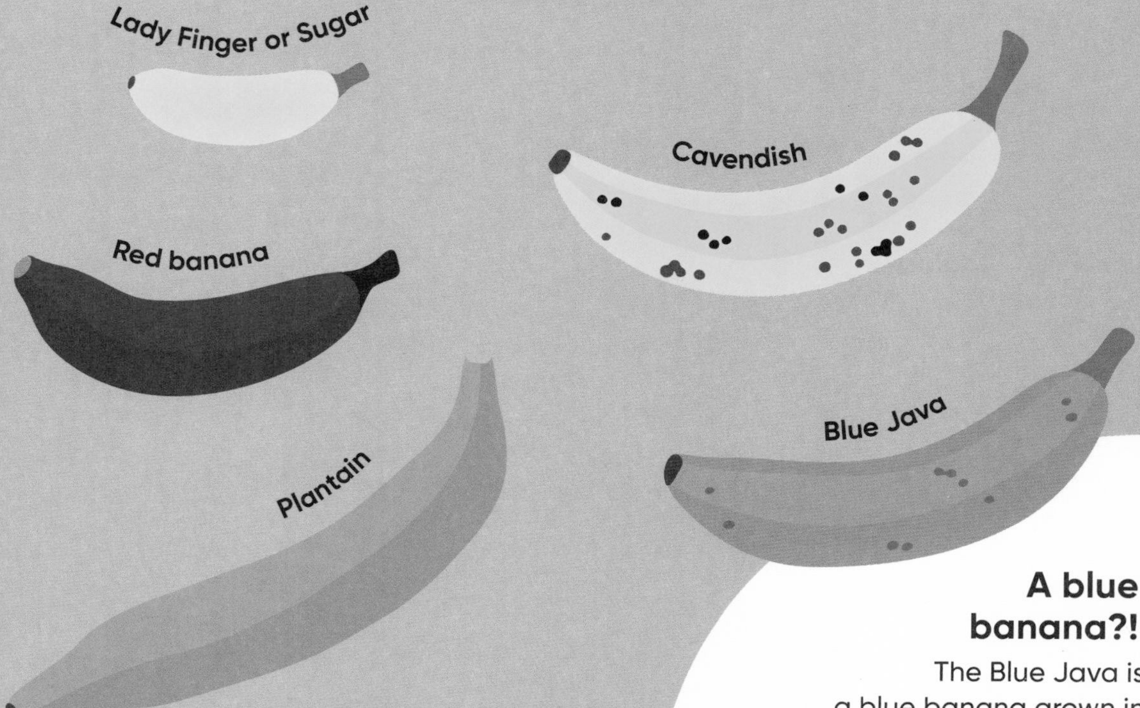

Lady Finger or Sugar

Cavendish

Red banana

Blue Java

Plantain

## A blue banana?!

The Blue Java is a blue banana grown in south Asia. Oddly, it tastes like vanilla ice cream.

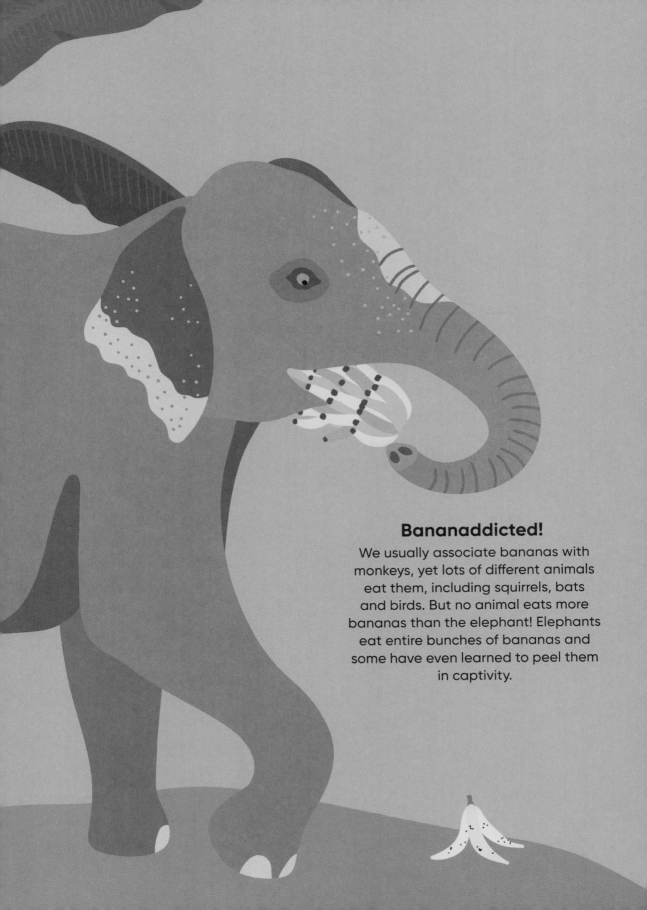

## Bananaddicted!

We usually associate bananas with monkeys, yet lots of different animals eat them, including squirrels, bats and birds. But no animal eats more bananas than the elephant! Elephants eat entire bunches of bananas and some have even learned to peel them in captivity.

## The happy fruit

Have you ever noticed the banana's curved shape looks like a smile? It's no surprise! Bananas contain an amino acid than is converted into serotonin in the brain. Serotonin is known as the happy hormone!

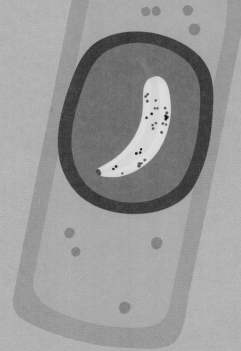

## Banana ketchup

In the Philippines, banana ketchup is a completely normal addition to any dish!

## Call it art!

In 2019, contemporary Italian artist Maurizio Cattelan created a work called *Comedian*, which was a real banana taped to a wall. It was widely ridiculed, but isn't art supposed to trigger a reaction? When it comes to art, anything goes!

# Oranges

This round fruit with a bumpy peel has been eaten for more than 2000 years. Cut into sections or squeezed into a juice, oranges are very popular!

Seed

Pulp

Thick, uneven rind

From flower to fruit

# A hybrid history

Most of the citrus fruits we know today are the result of genetic crossing carried out by humans throughout history.

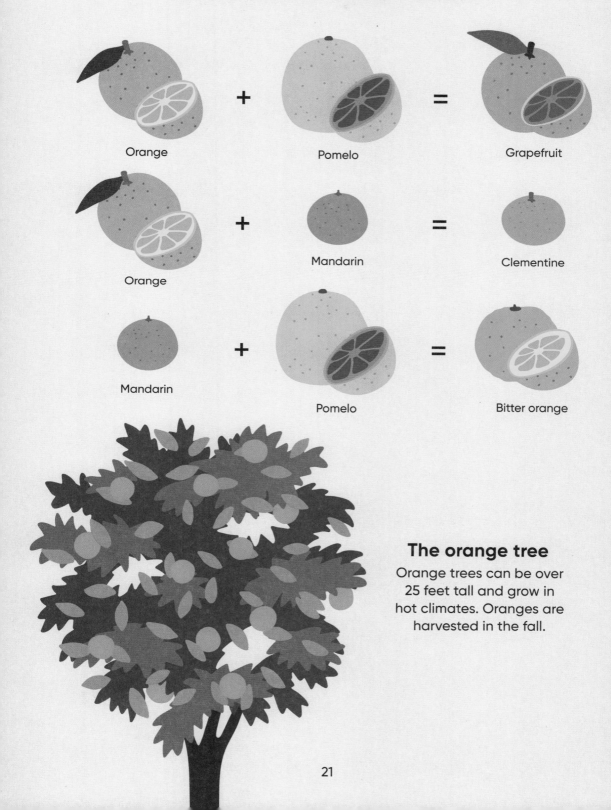

Orange + Pomelo = Grapefruit

Orange + Mandarin = Clementine

Mandarin + Pomelo = Bitter orange

## The orange tree

Orange trees can be over 25 feet tall and grow in hot climates. Oranges are harvested in the fall.

## A fruit and a color

Historically, the word "orange" first referred to the fruit and, later, to the color.

## An orange in a sock

Before the 1960s, getting an orange in your Christmas stocking was a good thing! At the time, oranges weren't all that common and quite expensive, so people really appreciated them.

## Mass production

The world's top orange producers are Brazil, India, China, Mexico, the United States, and Spain.

## The king of juices

Orange juice is rich in vitamin C and adds pep to any breakfast table! Three out of every four oranges grown in the world are used to make juice. It takes about ten to 15 oranges to make one quart of orange juice!

## Read the label

When it says "100% pure juice" on the label, it means the oranges were squeezed and the juice was pasteurized to stay fresh. "Made from concentrate" means some of the water was removed to make it easier to manufacture and ship. This step does remove some of the nutrients, but both types of juice are very good for you! The main thing to watch out for is added sugar or chemicals.

# Lemons

The lemon is a well-known citrus fruit. Its sour taste adds flavor and awakens the tastebuds! Lemons are grown throughout the world and are part of just about every culture's cuisine.

Rugged peel

Seed

Pulp

From flower to fruit

## Limes

Limes might look like green, unripe lemons, but they're actually a separate species.

## Black-bordered lemon moth

Some yellow animals have lemon in their name, like the black-bordered lemon moth and the lemon shark.

## A busy tree!

The lemon tree is a small evergreen shrub that can be ten to 16 feet tall. It produces lemons all year long.

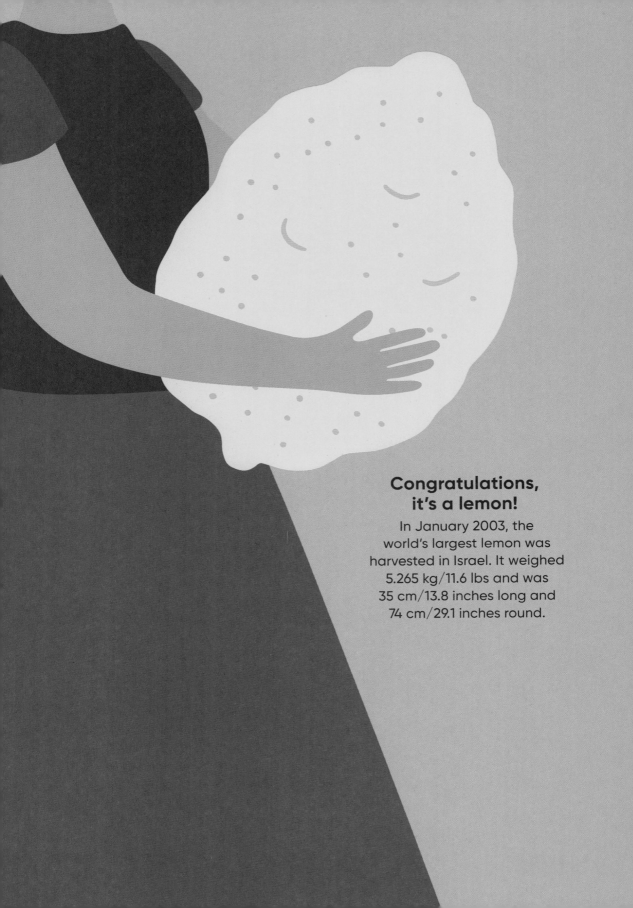

## Congratulations, it's a lemon!

In January 2003, the world's largest lemon was harvested in Israel. It weighed 5.265 kg/11.6 lbs and was 35 cm/13.8 inches long and 74 cm/29.1 inches round.

Lemon tart

Lemon cake

Lemonade

## Egyptian lemonade
Egyptians used to make a refreshing drink from barley, mint and lemon leaves. It was the ancient version of our lemonade!

Sorbet

Ravioli

# Strawberries

Starting in late spring/early summer, a heady scent tickles our noses
as we stroll through the market. It's strawberry time!
Bright red, juicy and ready to be devoured!

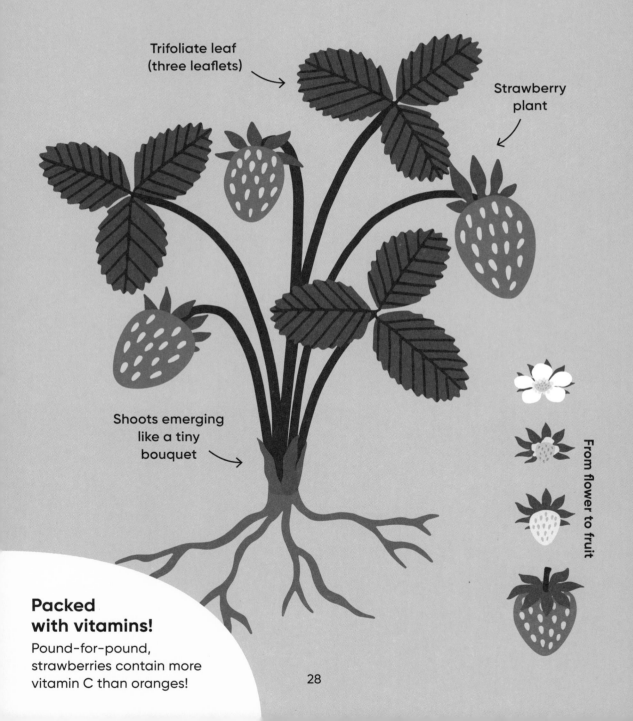

Trifoliate leaf
(three leaflets)

Strawberry
plant

Shoots emerging
like a tiny
bouquet

From flower to fruit

## Packed
## with vitamins!
Pound-for-pound,
strawberries contain more
vitamin C than oranges!

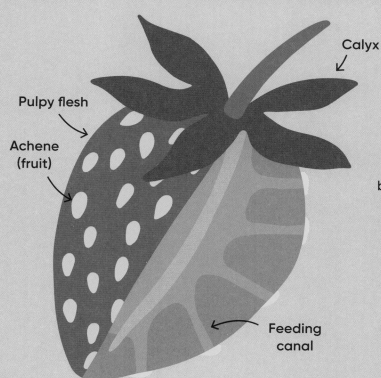

Calyx

Pulpy flesh

Achene
(fruit)

Feeding
canal

## A fruit
## within a fruit

The little yellow dots
on the surface are, in
botanical terms, the true
fruit of the strawberry
plant. These are called
achenes and each one
contains a tiny seed!

## A white
## strawberry!?

There is a variety of
strawberry with white flesh
and red seeds. Originally
from Chile, it's also called the
"pineberry" because it tastes
a bit like a pineapple!

## Jam or jelly?

When it comes to breakfast,
no fruit gets smattered on bread
as much as the strawberry.
Strawberry jam is made from
puréed strawberries cooked with
sugar. Strawberry jelly is made
by cooking the juice with sugar
and a thickener.

GIVE IT A TRY!

# "Pick" your fun!

Some strawberry growers open up their farms to people to pick their own strawberries right from the field. When the basket is full, the farmer weighs and the picker pays.

# Be the chef!

Learning to cook takes time, usually by trial and error.
One thing is for sure: Eating what you make yourself comes
with a sense of pride! It's often better for the environment
and you can save money, too.

# Apples

Native to central Asia, the apple is a superstar among fruits. Apples lend themselves to all sorts of recipes. Tart, mild or sweet, everyone has a favorite apple!

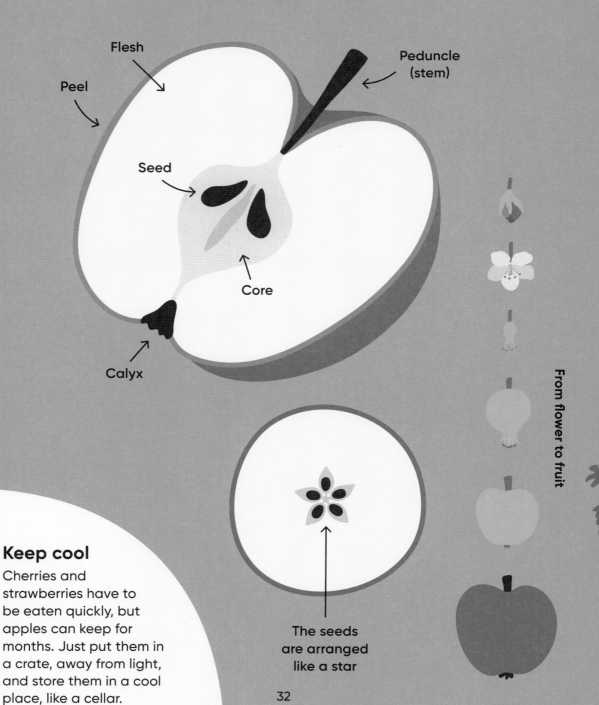

Flesh

Peel

Peduncle (stem)

Seed

Core

Calyx

The seeds are arranged like a star

From flower to fruit

## Keep cool

Cherries and strawberries have to be eaten quickly, but apples can keep for months. Just put them in a crate, away from light, and store them in a cool place, like a cellar.

# An apple rainbow

Gala

Granny Smith

Red Delicious

Golden

## Meet cousin Rose!

Apples and roses are cousins!
They're part of a family called
"Rosaceae." That's why apple
flowers that are starting to bud
look like tiny roses.

## A ripening agent

When apples are placed in a fruit
bowl with other fruit, they release
a gas called ethylene. This gas
causes the other fruit to ripen more
quickly! This is especially true of
ones that continue to ripen after
they're picked, such as lemons, kiwis,
avocados, and pears. If you don't
want them to ripen faster, separate
them from your apples.

Cider

Apple crumble

Apple strudel

Vinegar

Apple juice

Apple sauce

Candy apple

# Applicious!

Dried, squeezed or baked,
the juicy apple can be turned into
just about anything.

Apple flip

Apple chips

Apple pie

# Mushrooms

Mushrooms are neither plant nor animal. Their cellular makeup puts them in a kingdom all their own.

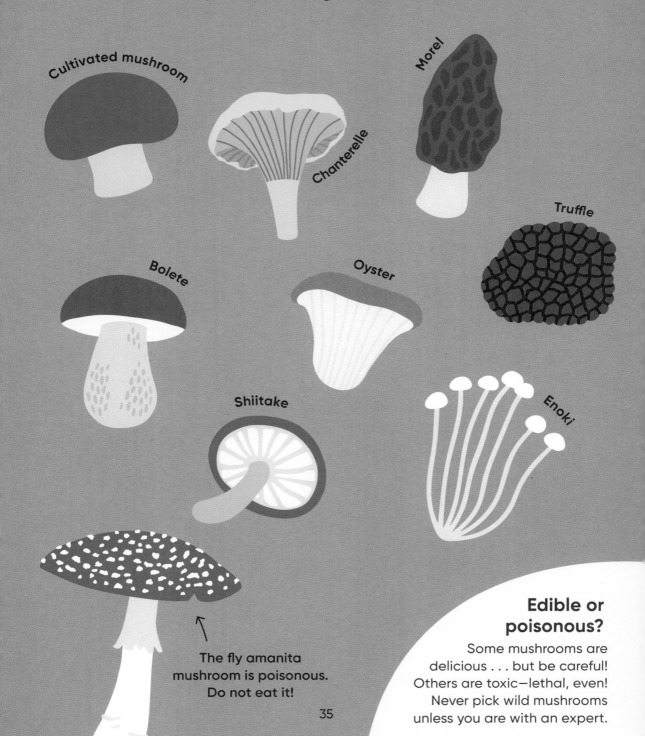

Cultivated mushroom

Chanterelle

Morel

Truffle

Bolete

Oyster

Shiitake

Enoki

The fly amanita mushroom is poisonous. Do not eat it!

### Edible or poisonous?

Some mushrooms are delicious . . . but be careful! Others are toxic—lethal, even! Never pick wild mushrooms unless you are with an expert.

# Tomatoes

With their juicy flesh and summery smell, tomatoes are delicious raw or cooked, tossed in a salad or simmering in a sauce. The tomato is native to South America.

Seeds

The stems and leaves are covered in tiny hairs and have a strong tomato smell.

From fruit to flower

# A large family

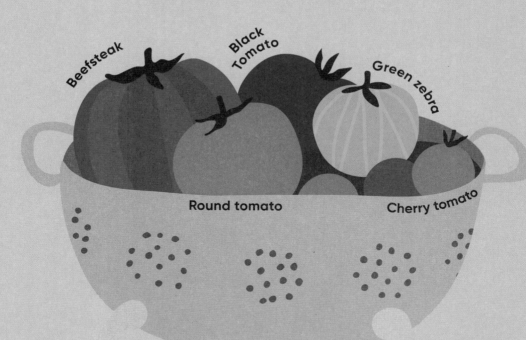

Beefsteak

Black Tomato

Green zebra

Round tomato

Cherry tomato

## A famous sauce

Tomato sauce is the most popular pasta sauce. And ketchup, made of sweetened tomato purée, is the number one fast-food condiment! Ketchup was already showing up in cookbooks in the early 1800s!

## The golden apple?

When the tomato was first brought to Naples, Italy, in 1554, it was called *pomodoro*, which means 'golden apple.' This means that the first imported tomatoes were most likely yellow!

# Fruit or vegetable?

Botanically speaking, the tomato is a fruit! In fact, almost all fleshy vegetables that have seeds are fruits! However, we often call it a vegetable because we use it in savory dishes.

# Homemade ketchup

GIVE IT A TRY!

Tomatoes

1

Vinegar

2  Salt

Nutmeg

Agave syrup

Paprika

3

4

1. Purée four nice, plump tomatoes (beefsteaks are a great choice). Place them in a pot.

2. Add 2 tablespoons of vinegar, 2 tablespoons of agave syrup (or sugar), 1 teaspoon of paprika, ½ teaspoon of salt and ½ teaspoon of nutmeg.

3. Let the mixture simmer over low heat for 20 minutes while stirring with a spatula. Let cool.

4. Serve your ketchup in a small bowl and store in the refrigerator.

# Pizza

According to surveys, pizza is the number one food for just about everyone, old and young. Enjoy it alfresco, make your own at home or have one delivered. Pizza is perfect for every occasion.

Base

Dough

Tomato sauce

Mozzarella

Seasonings

Pepper

Chili oil

Oregano

## Why do we call it "pizza"?

There are several theories. The word may come from the Greek word *pita*, which means 'cake.' Or it might come from the Latin *pinsa*, from the verb *pinsere*, meaning 'spread out' or 'flattened.'

40

Peppers

Mushrooms

Onion

Olives

Bacon

Jalapeños

Arugula

Ham

Pepperoni

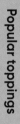
Popular toppings

## How do you like your pizza?

Maybe pizza is so popular because you can top it with your favorite things! Or maybe it's because you can eat it with your fingers. Or perhaps it's because every bite packs a flavor punch.

41

## Fit for a queen!

According to legend,
in 1889, Raffaele Esposito,
a *pizzaiolo* ('pizza maker'), was
tasked with making a pizza for the
Queen of Italy, Margherita of Savoy, who
was visiting Naples. He gave her three choices.
She opted for the one with the colors of the Italian flag:
fresh basil for the green, mozzarella for the white and tomato
sauce for the red. The pizzaiolo named it the margherita. Today,
the margherita is the most famous and best-selling type of pizza
(even though some people forget to add the basil!).

## Flying dough

*Pizzaioli* ('pizza makers') sometimes
perform acrobatic stunts with
their dough, spinning it above
their heads. In Italy, there are even
pizzaioli schools and competitions!
Not only is this technique fun for
restaurant patrons, but it also
stretches the dough and gives it
its round shape.

## Thick or thin?
Italian pizza is generally served with very thin crust. American pizza generally uses a thicker crust.

## To pineapple or not to pineapple?
It seems no one can agree on Hawaiian pizza! Some people love it; others find it an insult to traditional pizza. Contrary to popular belief, Hawaiian pizza was invented in Canada, not Hawaii!

## Hot, hot, hot!
Pizzas can be cooked in wood-fired ovens. At 400°C/750°F, they take barely a minute to cook!

# Onion and garlic

These are the two most commonly eaten bulbs in the world.
They bring life and add character to any dish.

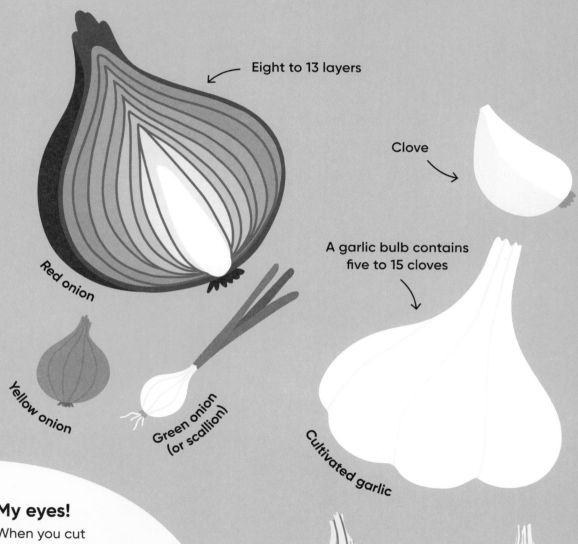

Eight to 13 layers

Clove

A garlic bulb contains
five to 15 cloves

Red onion

Yellow onion

Green onion
(or scallion)

Cultivated garlic

## My eyes!

When you cut
an onion, gases are
released that create an
acid when they come in
contact with the moisture in
our eyes. This causes our eyes
to burn and water! To avoid
this, place the onion in the
freezer for five minutes before
cutting it or rinse it in water.
Wear goggles if you have to!

Black garlic
(fermented
garlic)

Rosy garlic

Onion and garlic produce balls of countless, tiny flowers. They can be white or purple.

**Tip**
To get rid of the smell of garlic on your fingers, rub them against steel.

We eat the bulb of the plant, an underground organ that stores nutrients and energy.

# Eggplant

Native to South Asia, this funny-looking vegetable with dark-purple skin and spongy flesh has a rather bland taste. But when you cook with it, eggplant absorbs the flavors of the spices. The purple eggplant is the best known, but there are lots of varieties!

Seeds

Spongy flesh

Smooth, shiny skin

From flower to fruit

# A large family

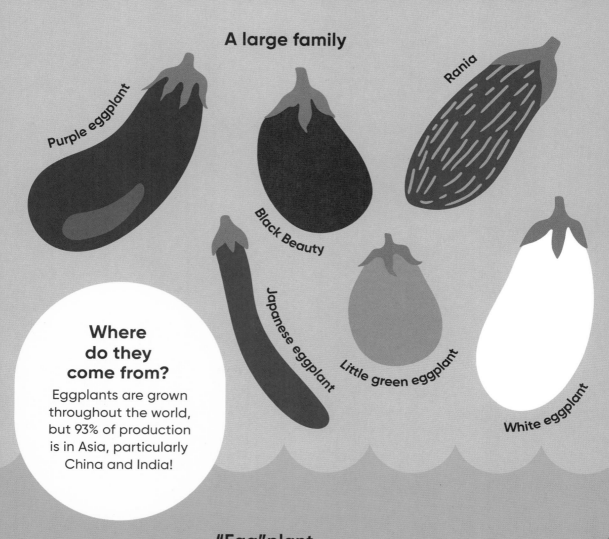

Purple eggplant

Black Beauty

Rania

Japanese eggplant

Little green eggplant

White eggplant

## Where do they come from?

Eggplants are grown throughout the world, but 93% of production is in Asia, particularly China and India!

## "Egg"plant

The name "eggplant" comes from a variety that is white and oval, like a hen's egg. Eggplants are sometimes called "aubergines," which comes from the French.

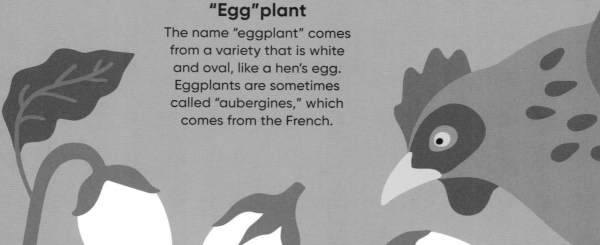

An egg-looking plant

# Carrots

If there is one vegetable popular with kids, it's the carrot!
Crunchy and sweet, carrots go well in any savory dish—salads,
curries or stews—as well as desserts, including carrot cake.

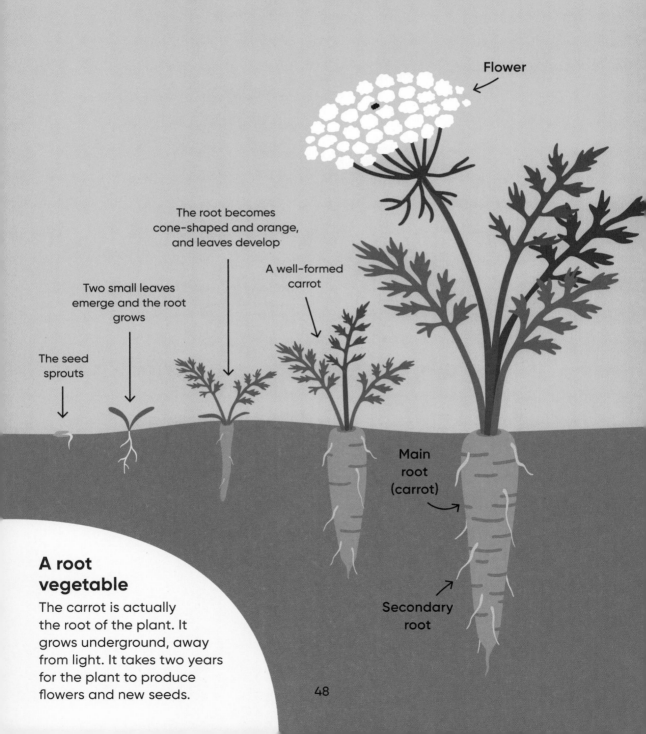

Flower

The root becomes
cone-shaped and orange,
and leaves develop

A well-formed
carrot

Two small leaves
emerge and the root
grows

The seed
sprouts

Main
root
(carrot)

Secondary
root

## A root vegetable

The carrot is actually
the root of the plant. It
grows underground, away
from light. It takes two years
for the plant to produce
flowers and new seeds.

48

## Are carrots *really* good for your eyes?

They sure are! Carrots are rich in vitamin A, which your eyes need to function properly, especially in low light. Unfortunately, carrots cannot fix a pre-existing issue with your eyes.

## A carrot rainbow

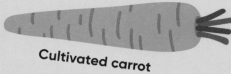

Cultivated carrot

White carrot

Red carrot

Cosmic purple

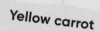

Yellow carrot

Black carrot

## How carrots got to be orange

Today, the orange carrot is the most famous of all. But it hasn't always existed! In 1500, it's believed that gardeners working for a powerful Dutch family named Orange-Nassau crossed yellow carrots with red carrots. This resulted in the orange carrot, a tribute to the family. Orange is the color of the Dutch royal family to this day.

## Carrots with a quirk

Usually, we pick the best-looking fruits and vegetables when we shop. But you're going to chop them up anyway, so does it really matter what they look like? Next time, add the odd-shaped ones to your basket so they don't get thrown out.

# At the market

Going to the market is a good way to support local farmers while reducing the environmental impact associated with transportation. It also helps reduce waste since there is no packaging. Fruits and vegetables that are only available in-season require less energy to grow than those grown in greenhouses. They're also more nutritious and better tasting, too!

# What about the other parts?

Sometimes, we discard the skin or another part of our fruits and vegetables . . .
Yet, these unused parts are often very nutritious!

Oven-roasted **cauliflower** leaves are delicious.

Every part of the **leek** and **Swiss chard** is edible.

**Cucumber** and **carrot** peels are loaded with vitamins.

## Should you wash your fruits and vegetables?

Fruits and vegetables may have come in contact with germs or chemicals (especially if they're not organic). That's why it's a good idea to wash them first.

## Why compost?

Composting at home (recycling the unused parts of your fruits and vegetables) returns nutrients to the soil and can be used for home heating.

**Broccoli** stems are very good!

# Anti-waste pesto

GIVE IT A TRY!

Nuts and seeds

Oil

Salt

Greens

Lemon

Garlic

1. Cut off your carrot and radish greens and place them in a blender.

2. Add 3 tablespoons of your favorite nuts and seeds, such as pine nuts, sunflower seeds and cashews.

3. Season with olive oil, salt, a clove of garlic and the juice from 1 lemon.

4. Blend and enjoy!

# Potatoes

Although potatoes have been farmed in South America for some 10,000 years, it wasn't until between the 16th and 18th centuries that they were introduced to the rest of the world.

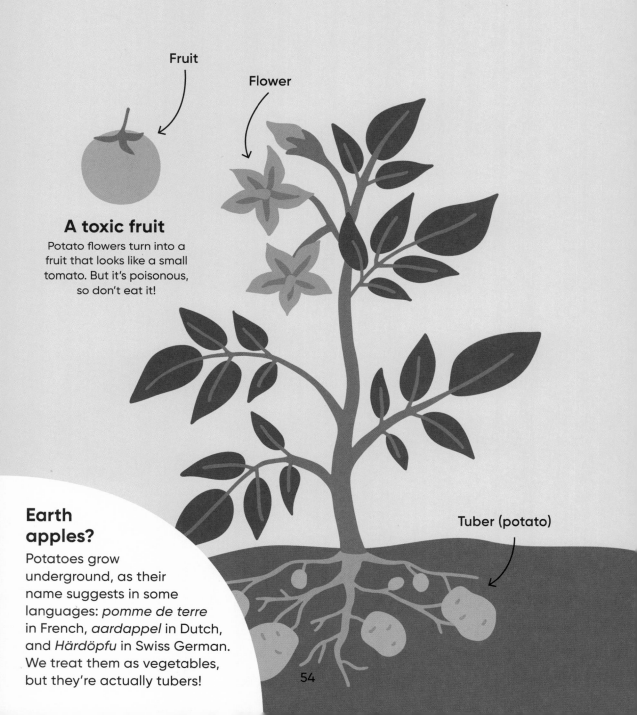

Fruit

Flower

## A toxic fruit

Potato flowers turn into a fruit that looks like a small tomato. But it's poisonous, so don't eat it!

Tuber (potato)

## Earth apples?

Potatoes grow underground, as their name suggests in some languages: *pomme de terre* in French, *aardappel* in Dutch, and *Härdöpfu* in Swiss German. We treat them as vegetables, but they're actually tubers!

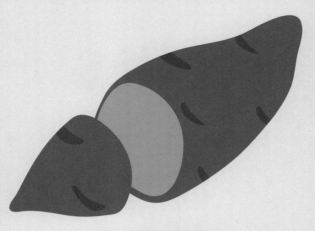

## Much sweeter!

With their purplish skin and orange flesh, sweet potatoes are softer and sweeter than potatoes. While often lumped together, these two tubers actually belong to different families.

## Water-logged!

A potato is 80% water!

## Space spuds!

In 1995, NASA successfully grew potatoes in space, aboard the Columbia space shuttle!

## Potato or spud?

People commonly call potatoes spuds. It appears the word comes from the name of a tool once used to dig holes for potato planting.

# French fries

Salty, crispy French fries are eaten around the world.
Served in a bag or a box, fries rule the fast-food world!

## A recipe
## for success

Making fries requires nothing
more than potatoes, oil
and salt. Fries are popular
worldwide because they're
easy and inexpensive.
Fries make great street food
and all you need are your
fingers. Nothing could
be simpler!

## Are French fries
## really French?

French fries probably originated in Belgium.
It was already customary for Belgians to fry
small fish. But when fish became scarce,
they substituted potatoes cut into sticks.
According to a more recent theory, French fries
were first made in Paris, along the Seine River,
toward the end of the 1700s. They would have
started as round slices, before eventually getting
their practical stick shape.

Traditional cut

## Come again!?

In the US, people say fries, but in the UK, they're chips. And when Americans say chips, they're referring to what the British call crisps. Got it?

Matchsticks

Wedges

Sliced potatoes

Crinkle cut

Sweet potato fries

## Fries around the world

France
*Moules-frites*
**(mussels and fries)**

United States
**Burger and fries**

England
**Fish 'n chips**

Belgium
*Cornet de frites*
**(fries in a cone)**

Quebec
*Poutine* **(fries with cheese curds and gravy)**

# Potato chips

They go "crunch" in your mouth and are probably the most popular snack in the world. Potato chips are salty and crispy, and everyone loves them. But how did slices of potato become so famous?

## Airbags?

Chip bags are filled with nitrogen to keep the chips from breaking. The gas also keeps them nice and crispy.

## How many potatoes does it take?

It takes around three pounds of potatoes to produce just one pound of potato chips! During the cooking process, the water evaporates and the potatoes lose two-thirds of their weight.

**Tortilla chips**
Made from corn and triangular

## A random invention

In 1853, an American cook named George Crum served fried potato slices to a customer. But the customer was very demanding and twice sent his food back to the kitchen because the potatoes weren't thin enough. Crum angrily sliced the potatoes a third time. This time, they were so thin they got extremely crispy! And that's how the first chips *may* have been invented. There are lots of different theories!

**Reconstituted chips**
They're all the same shape and come stacked in a tall can

**Corn puffs**
Flavors include cheddar and onion

## Can't eat just one!

When you put a chip in your mouth, its crispy texture is very satisfying. Chips combine three ingredients that trigger pleasure hormones: salt, sugar and fat. Our bodies need these, but only in small quantities. The problem is that it takes no time to eat a chip, so you have another and another and another . . . until you lose control! Unfortunately, chips are high in calories and eating too many can lead to health problems.

**Crinkle-cut chips**
The little ripples are good for catching the salt

**Rice crisps**
These come in a variety of flavors: ranch, sour cream, salt and vinegar, and so on

# Corn

This sweet-tasting, golden grain is native to Mexico. There, people have been eating it for 9000 years! Today, it's grown everywhere and there are thousands of varieties.

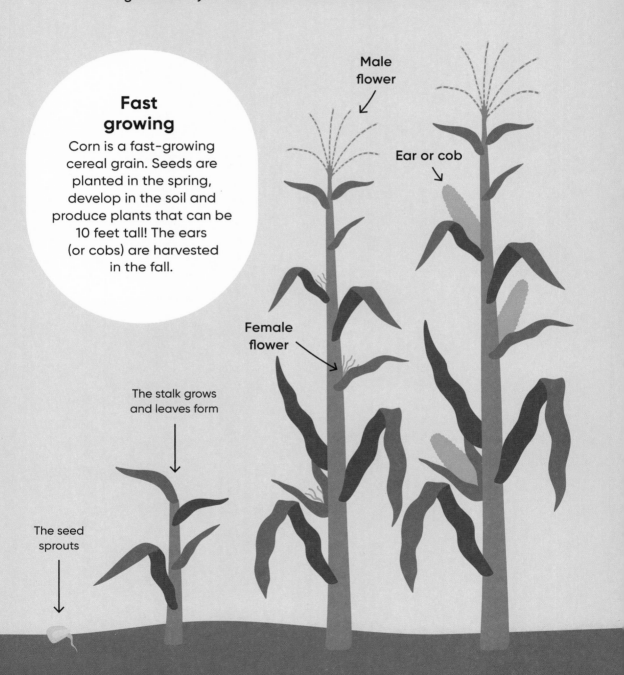

## Fast growing

Corn is a fast-growing cereal grain. Seeds are planted in the spring, develop in the soil and produce plants that can be 10 feet tall! The ears (or cobs) are harvested in the fall.

Male flower

Ear or cob

Female flower

The stalk grows and leaves form

The seed sprouts

# Top crop!

Corn is the most cultivated cereal grain in the world, ahead of wheat and rice. And it's not just grown for people. Corn is also used as animal feed and to make alcohol, glue, cosmetics, and much more.

## A cob of many colors!

In 1994, an American had the idea to cross several ancient varieties of different-colored corn. He was successful in growing a multi-colored corn called "rainbow" or "Glass Gem" corn!

## Corn creations

Tacos

Barbecued corn

Breakfast cereal

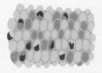

Popcorn

In a salad

Polenta (Italian cornmeal)

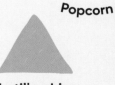
Tortilla chips

# Popcorn

Salty or sweet, the smell of popcorn has wafted through movie theaters for decades. But popcorn may have been invented by Native Americans. Archaeologists have found what they believe are popped corn grains in Aztec tombs!

## A magic cart

To the delight of passersby, American confectioner Charles Cretors invented an incredible cart for making popcorn in 1893. The cart could even roast peanuts and chestnuts and make coffee.

The type of corn used for making popcorn explodes at a temperature of 180°C/350°F.

**A corn kernel popping**

## Pop!

Corn kernels retain small amounts of water. When the kernels are heated, the water turns to steam. The steam pushes against the walls of the kernel, causing it to pop!

62

## Two shapes

When popcorn pops, it can have one of two shapes: butterfly, which also looks like a tooth or flower, and mushroom, which is completely round and is often used for popcorn that will be coated in chocolate or caramel. By crossing certain types of corn, we can produce popcorn that has only one shape or the other.

**Butterfly shape**

**Mushroom shape**

Even now, the red and white stripes on a popcorn box conjure up images of circus tents and wagons.

## What's a movie without popcorn?

In the early 1900s, popcorn carts were already a common sight at circuses and traveling theaters. But they weren't yet allowed in movie theatres. First, early films were silent and the sound of a neighbor munching and crunching on popcorn would have been distracting. Second, only high society went to the movies and they considered popcorn to be crude. However, popcorn stands were allowed outside movie theaters.

In the 1920s, going to the movies became more accessible to all. Finally, movie theaters caved in to popcorn's "pop"ularity and began selling it!

Today, popcorn and movies go hand-in-hand. Popcorn sales can account for as much as 50% of a theater's revenue!

# Squashes

Every fall, squashes make a big comeback. Out of the oven or in a soup, they're pure comfort food, with their sweet, tender pulp! There are many, many, many varieties of squashes.

Flower

Huge leaves

Tendril
(allows the plant to crawl, cling and climb)

From flower to fruit

Seeds

Pulp

## A hollow ring

If you want to know if your squash is ripe, just tap it. If you hear a hollow sound, it's ready to be eaten!

# A large family

Winter squash

Pattypan squash

Butternut squash

Musquée de Provence

Carnival squash

Zucchini

Longue de Nice

Summer squash

## Trick or treat!

Every October, pumpkins are hollowed out, given scary faces and lit from the inside. It's a jack-o'-lantern, so it must be Halloween!

Pumpkin

# Peppers

Peppers are native to South America, Central America and Mexico, so they need sun and heat to grow. Some varieties have a pungent (spicy or hot) taste, but all peppers make flavorful additions.

Peduncle (stem)

Seeds

From flower to fruit

## Red or green?

A pepper's color is an indication of its ripeness. Generally, peppers go from green (unripe) to red (ripe). But if they're picked before they're ripe, they keep their green (or orange or yellow) color.

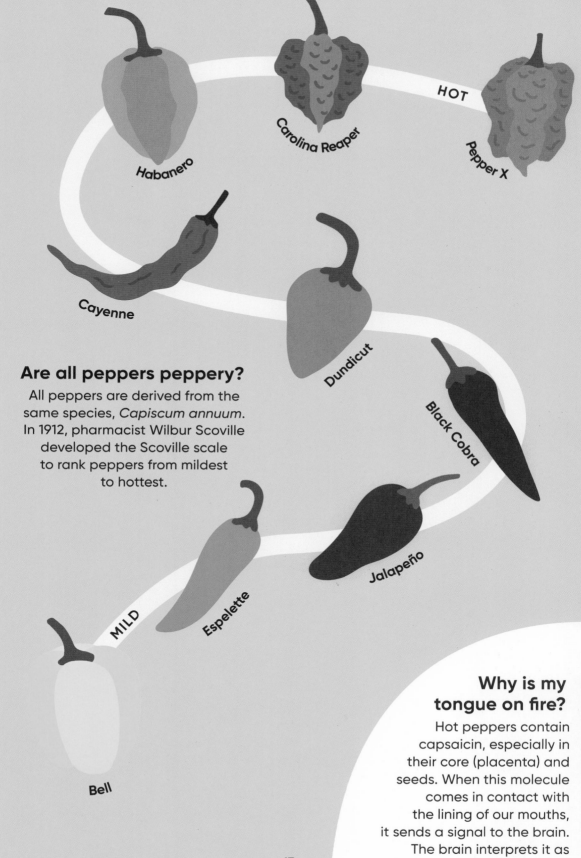

HOT

Carolina Reaper

Pepper X

Habanero

Cayenne

Dundicut

Black Cobra

## Are all peppers peppery?

All peppers are derived from the same species, *Capiscum annuum*. In 1912, pharmacist Wilbur Scoville developed the Scoville scale to rank peppers from mildest to hottest.

Jalapeño

Espelette

MILD

Bell

## Why is my tongue on fire?

Hot peppers contain capsaicin, especially in their core (placenta) and seeds. When this molecule comes in contact with the lining of our mouths, it sends a signal to the brain. The brain interprets it as a burning sensation.

## Doesn't hurt a bit!

The rose-ringed parakeet can eat
hot peppers because it's not sensitive
to pungency. So, this parrot
has nothing to fear.

# How to grow a pepper!

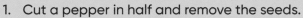

1. Cut a pepper in half and remove the seeds.

2. Fill a pot with soil and drop a few seeds on the surface. Cover them with 1 cm/⅓ in of soil. Keep the pot at room temperature on a windowsill that gets lots of sun.

3. Check the soil regularly and water when dry. For best results, plant the seeds between February and April so the plants are well-developed when the warm weather arrives.

4. After around 20 weeks, you should see small peppers appear.

# Cereal grains

Cereal grains are often eaten cooked or ground into flour.
They are part of a well-balanced diet.

Not gluten-free

Wheat

Oats

Rye

Barley

Spelt

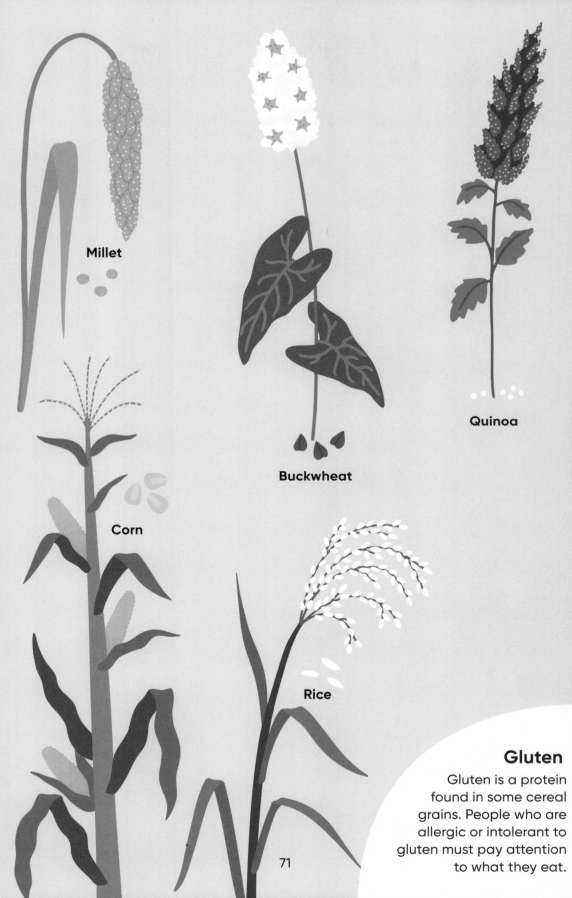

Millet

Corn

Buckwheat

Quinoa

Gluten-free

Rice

## Gluten

Gluten is a protein found in some cereal grains. People who are allergic or intolerant to gluten must pay attention to what they eat.

# Rice

Rice has been cultivated for 10,000 years and is a very nutritional and easily digestible food. It can be boiled or steamed or even ground into flour.

Rice grains form ears on the stems.

The grains of rice are protected by a thin outer layer. This husk (or hull) is removed for white rice but kept for brown rice. That's why brown has more nutrition.

## Wet feet?

Rice is a cereal grain that is grown in paddy fields—vast fields flooded with water. Although rice is grown around the world, 90% comes from Asia!

The rice plant takes root in soil submerged in water.

## Should rice be rinsed before cooking?

It all depends on what you want. For example, risotto should be a little sticky. But for basmati, you want the grains to separate. Rinsing rice removes the starch that makes the grains stick together.

## A large family

**Jasmine rice
Basmati rice**

**Wild rice**

**Red rice**

**Yellow rice**

**White rice
Risotto
Glutinous rice**

**Black rice**

**Sushi rice
Bomba rice (paella)
Rice for rice pudding**

Long-grain rice

Medium-grain rice

Short-grain rice

Paella

Cantonese fried rice

Sushi

Risotto

Rice noodles

Mochi

Rice cake

Biryani

## A very important food

Rice is one of the most commonly eaten cereal grains in the world. More than half the world's population eats it with nearly every meal!

# Sushi

Starting in the 1990s, sushi began to conquer the world.
This traditional Japanese dish is often served with soy sauce,
ginger and wasabi. There are hundreds of varieties!

Sheet of nori
(dried seaweed)

Filling (vegetables, egg,
fish, avocado, etc.)

Rice

Maki

The rice is covered with
a piece of salmon
or other fish.

Nigiri

Sashimi

Piece of
raw fish

Uramaki

The filling is wrapped
in rice and sesame
seeds.

Tamagoyaki

Temaki

The rice is covered
with a small omelet
held in place with a
small strip of nori.

The rice and filling are
rolled into a sheet of nori,
forming a cone.

## Origin of the word "sushi"

In Japanese, *su*
means 'vinegar' and *shi*
means 'rice.' Sushi rice is
prepared with rice vinegar
to add flavor.

# What goes with sushi?

**Soy sauce** for dipping.
It can be salty or sweet.

**Ginger** is eaten between different sushis
to cleanse the palette.

**Wasabi** is a very pungent paste made from
the plant of the same name, which is a cousin
of horseradish. In fact, much of the wasabi we
eat is just colored horseradish.

## The ancestor of sushi

An ancient recipe called
"nare-zushi" involved
fermenting fish in salt rice.
The rice was then discarded.
It's only when the use of
vinegar was introduced that
the rice was considered part
of the dish. If this dish is the
ancestor of sushi, then sushi
is not from Japan but from
various parts of Southeast
Asia!

Master sushi chef hat

## A patient profession

It takes a decade of experience
to become a master sushi chef!
In the first few years, apprentices are
not allowed to cut the fish or even cook
the rice! Instead, they do small jobs
and observe the masters.

The santoku is a special knife used for
cutting sushi. It doesn't stick to the sushi
thanks to little dimples in the blade.

# Bread

Bread is a universal product and people everywhere have been eating it for centuries. It's part of our everyday lives and can make a special occasion even more special. Bread is quite simply at the heart of our culinary traditions.

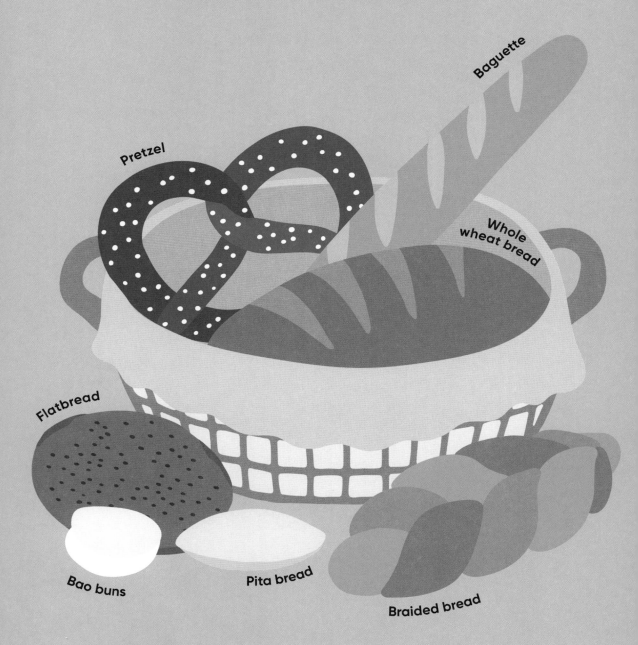

Baguette

Pretzel

Whole wheat bread

Flatbread

Bao buns

Pita bread

Braided bread

# Four simple ingredients

### Flour

gives the bread its texture, as well as its taste and color. It's the key ingredient!

### Yeast

reacts with the sugars in the flour and creates carbon dioxide. This gas causes the bread to rise.

### Salt

adds flavor and gives the bread a nice crust as it bakes.

### Water

acts as a binding agent.

## Making a toast

When we toast someone, we raise our glasses in their honor. The expression may date back to ancient times when spiced bread was toasted and added to drinks for flavor.

## The invention of the sandwich

In 1762, John Montagu, the Earl of Sandwich in England, asked his cook to prepare him a simple meal he could nibble on while playing cards. The cook served him meat and cheese between two slices of bread. The snack was a hit and became a regional specialty named after the Earl.

## In the wee, wee hours

At 3:00 a.m., the alarm goes off. While everyone else is still snuggled in their beds, bakers are already up and at 'em! The first task is to make the bread dough. After the dough is kneaded, it's set aside to slowly rise. While they wait, the bakery staff makes pastries and cakes. When the dough is ready, it's time to form the shapes. These are weighed for consistency. The dough rises a second time and little cuts are made so it rises properly and looks nice and pretty. Then, in the oven they go! When they're done, the breads have to cool before they can be sold—but not too much, because customers love nice, warm bread! The various breads are placed in the windows for display and the bakery can open!

# French toast

Milk

Sugar

Cinnamon

Egg

① ②

Sliced stale bread

③

④

1. Pour a cup of milk (or plant-based beverage) into a mixing bowl and add 2 tablespoons of sugar, a pinch of cinnamon and an egg (if you wish). Mix well.

2. Place the stale bread slices in the mixture and let them soak for a few minutes.

3. Place your bread in a lightly greased pan and cook until golden, around 5 minutes on each side.

4. Throw a few red berries on top for pizzazz!

# Pasta and noodles

As a side dish, baked with cheese or topped with a sauce, pasta and noodles are inexpensive, simple to prepare and lend themselves to all sorts of delicious recipes. To make them, all you need is flour, water, salt, and sometimes egg. It's that easy!

Penne

Farfalle

Elbow

Rigatoni

Macaroni

Gnocchi

Shell

Tortellini

Fusilli

Ravioli

Gyoza
Japanese dumpling

Jiǎozi
Chinese dumpling

Manti
Turkish dumpling

Pierogi
Polish dumpling

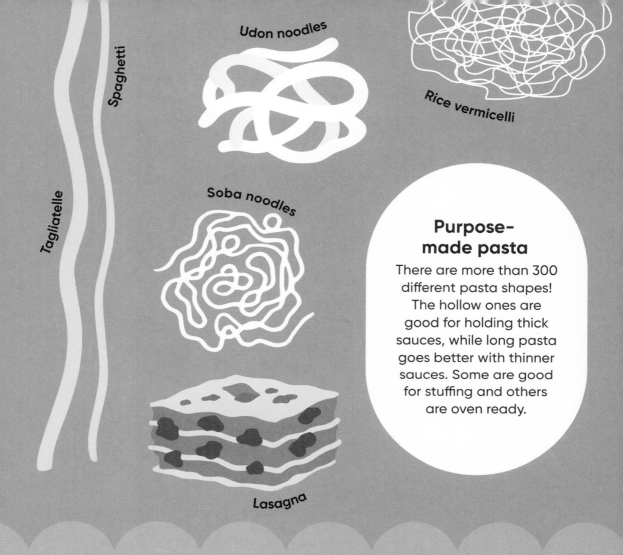

Spaghetti

Tagliatelle

Udon noodles

Rice vermicelli

Soba noodles

## Purpose-made pasta

There are more than 300 different pasta shapes! The hollow ones are good for holding thick sauces, while long pasta goes better with thinner sauces. Some are good for stuffing and others are oven ready.

Lasagna

## A pasta rainbow

The flour used can determine the color. And during production, naturally colored ingredients can also be added.

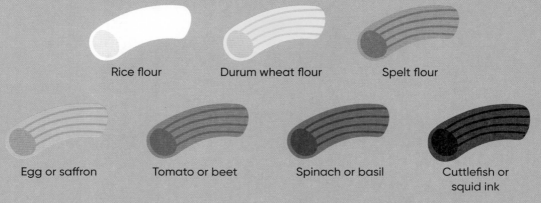

Rice flour

Durum wheat flour

Spelt flour

Egg or saffron

Tomato or beet

Spinach or basil

Cuttlefish or squid ink

## Dry pasta or fresh pasta?

Dry pasta comes from removing the moisture during production. This gives them a longer life and makes it easier to get them to market. Dry pasta takes around ten minutes to cook. With fresh pasta, there is still water in the dough. Fresh pasta can keep for four or five days at most, and cooking time is only two to four minutes.

## Al dente!

In Italian, *al dente* means 'to the tooth.' When it comes to pasta, this culinary term is what you're after: tender but slightly firm to the bite. For Italians, eating overcooked pasta is virtually a crime!

## Chinese or Italian?

This is a debate for the ages! There are tales of Marco Polo bringing noodles back to Italy from China. It is true that the oldest evidence of noodles was discovered in China, dating back some 4000 years. But according to fossil evidence from Greece and the Middle East, many types of pasta were being cooked well before Marco Polo's travels. If the birthplace is hard to pin down, one thing is for sure: the Italians have all their different types of pasta and the Chinese have their noodles!

## Slurp!

In Japan, slurping while you eat your noodles is a compliment to the chef. It means you enjoyed them! Making noise while you eat would be seen as impolite in other countries!

# Chocolate

It's smooth and creamy and melts in your mouth . . .
who doesn't like chocolate? Even though this treat requires
considerable effort to make, people everywhere love chocolate.

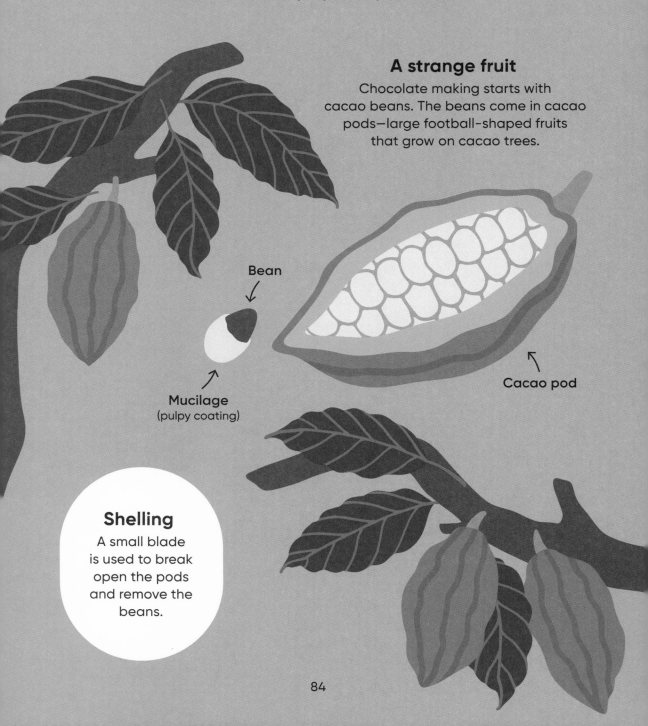

## A strange fruit

Chocolate making starts with
cacao beans. The beans come in cacao
pods—large football-shaped fruits
that grow on cacao trees.

Bean

Mucilage
(pulpy coating)

Cacao pod

## Shelling

A small blade
is used to break
open the pods
and remove the
beans.

## Growing a cacao tree

Cacao trees grow in tropical climates near the equator, in places like Asia and Latin America. But the most cacao beans are harvested in Africa, especially Côte d'Ivoire and Ghana. The trees are not easy to grow, as they need lots of moisture and shade. Plus, only one in every 500 flowers produces a pod!

The pods grow directly on the trunk or main branches. When they're ripe, red pods turn orange and green ones turn yellow.

## Cocoa, an ancient beverage

The Aztecs drank a beverage made from crushed cacao beans, spices, and water. They called it *xocoatl*, meaning 'bitter water.' This word may be where the word "chocolate" comes from. It wasn't until cacao was brought to Europe that sugar was added by the upper classes to make it less bitter.

# How a bean becomes a bar

**1**

The pods are **harvested** in Africa, South America or Indonesia.

**2**

The beans are **fermented** in barrels.

**3**

The **beans** are dried in the sun.

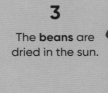

**4**

The beans are **shipped** by boat or plane to countries in the Northern Hemisphere (Europe, United States, Japan, etc.).

**5**

The beans are **roasted**, which allows the flavors to develop.

**6**

The beans are **ground** to produce cacao paste. The paste can also be pressed to separate the cacao butter from the dry matter, which is used to make cocoa powder.

**7**

Through a process known as **conching**, the cacao paste is **mixed** with sugar, cacao butter and milk until it is consistent.

**8**

The chocolate is **tempered** by melting the cacao paste to specific temperatures to obtain a smooth, shiny texture.

**9**

Liquid chocolate is **poured into a mold**, where it cools and hardens.

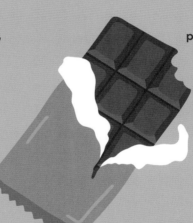

**10**

The chocolate is **packaged** and can now be sold and enjoyed!

### Dark chocolate

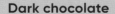

Is made with cacao paste, sugar and cacao butter.

### Milk chocolate

Is made with cacao paste, sugar, cacao butter, and powdered milk.

### White chocolate

Is made with cacao butter, sugar and powdered milk. This chocolate contains no cacao paste, which explains why it is white!

# Hazelnut spread

Hazelnuts

②

③

Coconut oil

④

Milk

Cocoa powder

Sugar

Salt

⑤

1. Arrange 150 g/5 oz of hazelnuts on a baking sheet and roast for 10 minutes at 180°C/350°F. Remove from the oven and let cool.

2. Rub the hazelnuts with a cloth to remove loose pieces of skin.

3. Blend the hazelnuts in a food processor until a smooth purée forms.

4. Add 2 tablespoons of cocoa, 1 tablespoon of sugar (skip if your cocoa is pre-sweetened), 3 tablespoons of coconut oil, 1 tablespoon of milk (or plant-based milk) and a pinch of salt. Blend again!

5. Scoop the spread into a small jar. It can be stored at room temperature for around a week.

# Nut parmesan

GIVE IT A TRY!

Nuts and seeds ①

Nutritional yeast ②

Salt

③

④

1. Grind 150 g/5 oz of your favorite nut or seed (e.g., cashews or sunflower seeds) in a blender.

2. Add 3 tablespoons of nutritional yeast and 1 teaspoon of salt.

3. Blend again to a fine powder.

4. Pour the nut parmesan into a jar. It can keep at room temperature for several weeks. Sprinkle over pasta, crepes or risotto!

# Nuts and seeds

Hazelnuts

Walnuts

Almonds

Pistachios

Chestnuts

Pecans

Peanuts

Brazil nuts

Macadamia nuts

Cashews

Coconuts

Cashews are the seeds of the cashew tree. The nut forms at the end of the cashew apple—a fruit-like, pear-shaped plant.

Squash seeds/ Pepitas

Sunflower seeds

Sesame seeds

Sesame is a plant that sports pretty, light-pink flowers. Their tiny seeds vary from black to white.

Chia seeds

Have you ever noticed that chia seeds look like tiny dinosaur eggs?

## So versatile!

Nuts and seeds can be eaten raw or roasted. They're great in salads or for making oil or butter. They're good for you and are high in protein, iron, vitamins, and fiber. They're also pleasing to the eye, so throw some on your plate!

Pine nuts

Pine nuts are seeds found in the cones of some pine trees.

Flax seeds

Flax flowers turn into fruit that house the seeds.

# Legumes

Legumes come in many different forms and have many different tastes. They're super rich in protein and have lots of fiber. A plate without a legume . . . well, it's plain wrong.

## Peas or beans?

They're from the same family, but you can tell them apart like this: beans have oval seeds, whereas peas have round seeds.

Pod

Garden peas

Seed (pea)

Snow peas

Also known as the mange-tout (from French), this pea comes from the same plant as the garden pea, but its pods are picked before the peas are ripe.

Soybeans

Chickpeas

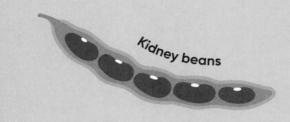
Kidney beans

**Navy beans**

**Black beans**

Green beans

## Peas in a pod
The edible seeds of legumes form inside pods that look like little sleeping bags. The number of seeds per pod can vary greatly!

**Brown lentils**

**Green lentils**

**Black lentils**

**Red lentils**

Each pod has two lentils (lens-shaped seeds).

# Tofu

Tofu has been made in Asia for a very long time. In recent years, more and more cultures around the world have started using it.

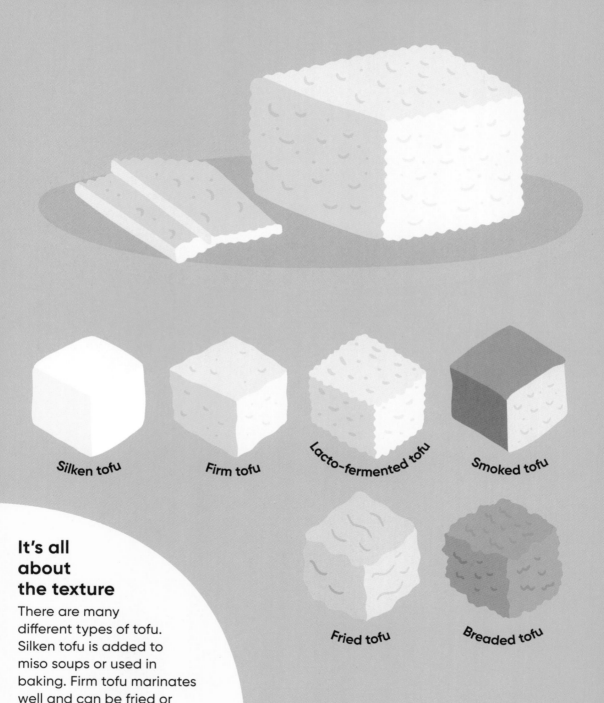

Silken tofu

Firm tofu

Lacto-fermented tofu

Smoked tofu

Fried tofu

Breaded tofu

## It's all about the texture

There are many different types of tofu. Silken tofu is added to miso soups or used in baking. Firm tofu marinates well and can be fried or breaded.

# Making tofu

**1**

Soybeans and water are **blended** to produce a soy liquid.

**2**

The liquid is **curdled** by adding calcium sulfate and bittern (or nigari, a salt solution used for hardening).

**3**

The liquid and clots resulting from curdling are **pressed** to form a solid block.

Pad Thai

Scrambled tofu

Tofu burger

Tofu nuggets

Skewers

## Guess what!

The first time you try tofu, you might think it's bland and spongy. But there are a thousand ways to cook it and each way has a different taste.

## An alternative to meat

Tofu is a main feature in vegetarian and vegan diets. It's a good way to lower our meat consumption and is packed with protein.

Custard

# Condiments

**Pepper**
Comes from the piper (or pepper) plant, which is a vine. The berries are dried and ground.

**Salt**
Comes from seawater or is extracted from rock salt.

**Soy sauce**
Is made from the seeds of soy and wheat.

**Oil**

Comes from pressing foods such as olives, walnuts, sunflower seeds, rapeseed, or flax seed.

**Vinegar**

Comes mainly from grapes but also from apples, rice, dates, figs, and so on.

**Mustard**

Comes from the seeds of the mustard plant.

**Mayonnaise**

Is a mixture of oil, eggs, vinegar, mustard, and lemon.

# Spices

### Paprika
Comes from drying and crushing peppers.

### Cumin
Is an oriental plant with a very strong fragrance. The seeds are crushed or used whole.

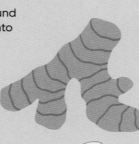

### Turmeric
Is a plant whose rhizomes (underground roots) are ground into a powder.

### Ginger
Can be used fresh or powdered. It comes from the rhizomes of the plant, just like turmeric. The two plants look similar.

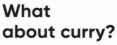

### Saffron
Comes from the red stigma of the crocus flower. Saffron adds flavor and a lovely golden hue to whatever you're making.

## What about curry?
Curry is not a single spice, but a combination of spices, including coriander, cumin and turmeric.

### Nutmeg

Can be ground into a powder or grated. It adds character to purées, sauces and soups.

### Cinnamon

Comes from the tree of the same name. Strips of bark are peeled off and dried.

### Star anise

Is a very fragrant dry fruit with a festive flavor used for making mulled wine at Christmas. It is also used in Asian broths and Indian beverages.

### Vanilla bean

Is the fruit of the vanilla orchid. The minuscule seeds are removed with a knife and added as a sweet flavoring.

### Cardamom

Is a plant that resembles an orchid. The seeds are used whole or ground.

# Herbs

Thyme

Basil

Dill

Parsley

Chives

Sage

Rosemary

Oregano

Cilantro/ Coriander

Mint

# Plant-based milks

Soy

Coconut

Oat

### Who's it for?
Plant-based milks are mainly consumed by people who are lactose intolerant or who prefer not to drink animal milk for environmental or ethical reasons.

Rice

Almond

# Sugar

There's no escaping sugar! You'll find it in soft drinks, cookies and candy, as well as in fruits and cereals. But not all sugars have the same effect on our bodies!

### Is sugar bad?
Our bodies need sugar for energy. It's like fuel! But too much sugar can cause health problems, such as tooth decay, obesity and diabetes. It's all about moderation!

## Natural sugar and added sugar

Some foods naturally contain sugar, such as fruit, milk and even pasta! But candy, cookies and sodas are made with added sugars. No one type, natural or added, is better or worse than the other. The difference lies in the food it's contained in: A piece of fruit has sugar and also fiber and vitamins, but a cookie has a lot of sugar and few nutrients, which is not ideal for your health.

# From beet to sugar

**1**

Sugar beet is **harvested** from the fields.

**2**

The beet is brought to a factory, where it is **washed and cut** into pieces.

**3**

The pieces are **steeped** in hot water to produce a syrup.

**4**

The water **evaporates**, leaving behind sugar that is then crystallized.

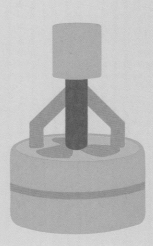

**5**

The sugar is **spun** in a large basket, called a centrifuge, to dry out.

**6**

The sugar is ready to be **conditioned** and sent to market, where it is sold as a powder or in cubes!

## Two plants

White sugar comes from the root of the sugar beet plant or from sugarcane, a species of tall grass resembling a reed. Cane sugar comes only from sugarcane. In nutritional terms, there is no difference between these sugars. Sugarcane molasses is used as an additive to make brown sugar.

# Ice cream

Summer is here! It's time for shorts and T-shirts, beach days, longer evenings, and family vacations . . . But more than anything, it's time to beat the heat with some refreshing ice cream!

Bowl

Cone

Sundae

Ice cream bar

Ice pop

Sorbet

Gelato

Spiral

Ice cream sandwich

## Would you like some cream with that?

Ice cream is made with cream, milk and even eggs. Sorbets and ice treats are not really ice creams, as they are made with water.

104

## A stroke of luck

In 1905, an 11-year-old boy named Frank Epperson made himself a soda and mixed it with a wooden stick. He forgot about his drink and left it outside, and it froze overnight. When he grabbed his soda-turned-ice cube by the stick, he discovered it was delicious! The frozen treat on a stick was born! When he was 18, he patented the idea and started his own company.

## The first sorbet?

In ancient times, Roman emperor Nero demanded there be ice on his dinner table—winter, summer, it didn't matter! His servants were forced to scale mountains to fetch the fresh snow needed for the ice. To keep the snow from melting along the way, they would wrap it in fur. They added fruit and honey, creating something similar to today's sorbet.

# Snow ice cream

Milk

Snow

① ② ③

Vanilla extract

Sugar

1. Collect a bowlful of clean, freshly fallen snow.

2. In another bowl, whisk ½ teaspoon of vanilla extract, 1 tablespoon of sugar and 8 tablespoons of very cold milk (or plant-based beverage).

3. Add the snow, bit by bit, stirring gently until it has the consistency of ice cream. Enjoy!

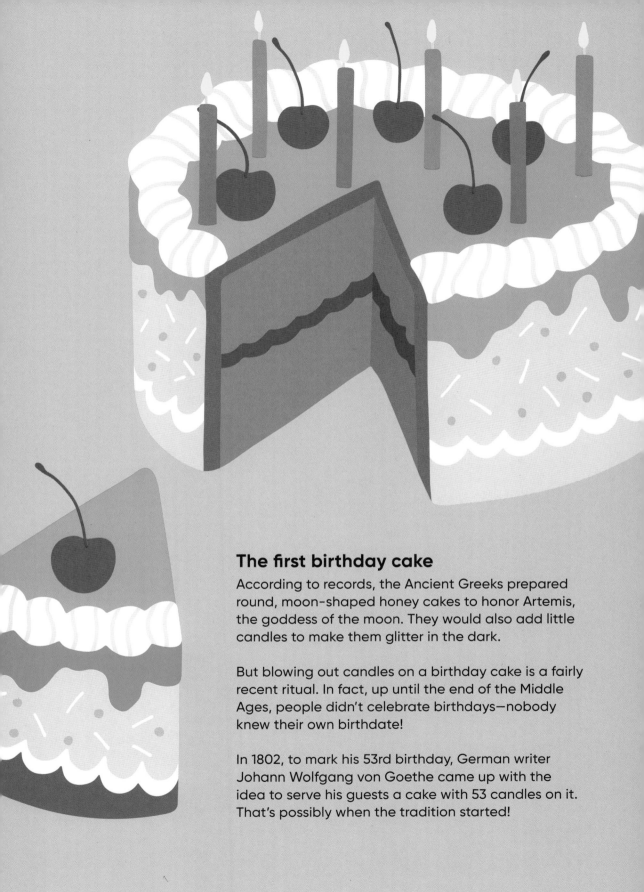

## The first birthday cake

According to records, the Ancient Greeks prepared round, moon-shaped honey cakes to honor Artemis, the goddess of the moon. They would also add little candles to make them glitter in the dark.

But blowing out candles on a birthday cake is a fairly recent ritual. In fact, up until the end of the Middle Ages, people didn't celebrate birthdays—nobody knew their own birthdate!

In 1802, to mark his 53rd birthday, German writer Johann Wolfgang von Goethe came up with the idea to serve his guests a cake with 53 candles on it. That's possibly when the tradition started!

# Beverages

### Water

It's the purest drink of all.
We get drinking water from
rain, the ground, glaciers,
lakes, and so on.

### Iced tea

The king of summer drinks!
The recipe is the same as
for regular hot tea, except
we drink it cold. Unless it's
homemade, iced tea often
contains a lot of sugar.

### Fruit juice

Orange, apple or
grapefruit . . . juices are
good sources of energy.

### Soft drinks

Made from carbonated water,
sugar and flavors that are
sometimes extracted from plants
but often artificial. Other names
include pop, soda and soda pop—
what it's called usually depends on
where you live.

### Lemonade

Is made with water,
lemon juice and sugar.
Lemonade can be fizzy
or flat.

### Syrup

Made from fruit, sugar and (often)
artificial flavors. Syrup is mixed
with water and can be just about
any color.

## Refreshments

# Hot beverages

## Hot chocolate
Is made from cocoa powder and milk. Whipped cream makes a nice topping.

## Tea
Comes from steeping the dried leaves of the tea shrub (Camellia sinensis) in hot water.

## Coffee
We get coffee from the beans of the coffee tree, which are roasted, ground and mixed with water. Only adults should drink coffee because it stimulates the nervous system.

## Infusions
These are herbal teas, made from leaves, flowers or fruit steeped in hot water.

## Milk
Can come from cows, goats or sheep, or it can be replaced with plant-based milks.

## Winter warmers!
When it's cold outside, there's nothing better than a steaming cup of tea or hot chocolate to warm your bones. Grab your mug and a cookie, throw a log on the fire and watch the snow fall outside.

# Animal products

So far, this book has helped you learn more about the many different foods we get solely (or mainly) from plants. But animal products are also a big part of the food we eat.

Dairy products

Yogurt

Cheese

Feta

Milk

Mozzarella

Butter

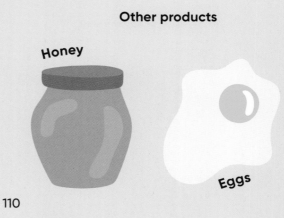

Other products

Honey

Eggs

## Is cheese addictive?

Eating dairy, such as cheese, can create a feeling of comfort. And some of us just can't get enough! There is a biological explanation for this: milk contains casein, a protein designed to be addictive for babies. And for good reason—it's for their own survival! This craving for the comfort of dairy can extend into adulthood!

110

Chicken legs and wings

Chicken

Chicken nuggets

## Two words, same thing

The names for the meat we eat are sometimes different than the names of the animals they come from. For instance, beef comes from cows and pork comes from pigs. But chicken, well, comes from chickens.

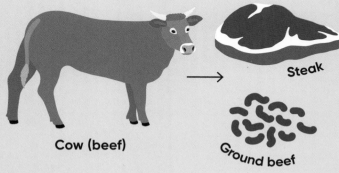

Steak

Cow (beef)

Ground beef

## Why is there pork in candy?

Sometimes, companies add a pork- or beef-based gelatin to their candy. Check for these codes in the ingredient list: E428 and E441.

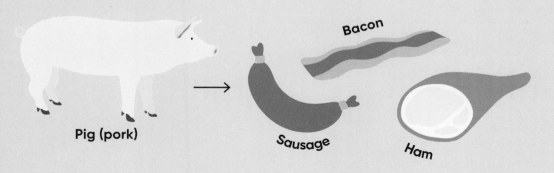

Bacon

Pig (pork)

Sausage

Ham

Meat products

Seafood

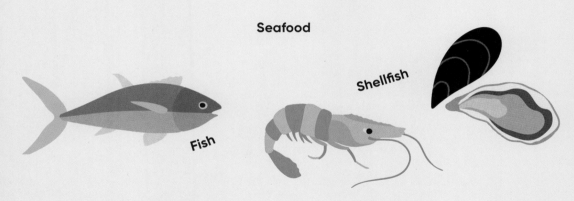

Shellfish

Fish

# The kitchen!

The kitchen is a magical place, where ingredients are transformed into mouth-watering meals, tempting treats and succulent soups!

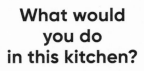

### What would you do in this kitchen?

Would you grab a hunk of cheese from the fridge? Or a cookie from the shelf? What tasty ingredients would you throw in the soup?

# Awaken your senses!

## Taste

This sense tells us what we like and dislike. Sweet, sour, salty, or bitter . . . there is no end to the flavors.

## Sight

The glistening crust of a croissant, the roundness of a donut . . . appetite has a lot to do with how appealing something looks!

## Sound

A knife slicing through a zucchini and going thud on the cutting board, butter sizzling in a pan, a chip going "crunch" in your mouth . . . sound is a big part of our culinary experience!

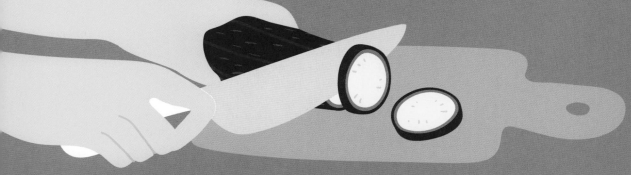

## Smell

A simmering soup, the exotic aroma of a mango . . . when something smells good, it makes us hungry and tells us a good deal about its quality.

## Food and emotions

How do you feel when you think of a peach, a croissant, a potato or a tomato? Does it make you hungry or does it "gross you out"? Do you feel surprised, happy or curious? Different foods can trigger different emotions.

## Touch

The soft, velvety skin of an apricot, the furry feel of a kiwi . . . our sense of touch is stimulated when we cook or eat with our fingers.

# Allergies and intolerances

Every body is different and each of us has our own genetic makeup.
So, sometimes, some of us cannot eat certain foods. But why?

## Allergies

The human body has a number of astonishing ways to defend itself. Allergy symptoms range from blotchy skin, which is uncomfortable, to breathing problems, which is more serious. There are many common allergens, including peanuts, gluten, fruit, eggs, mustard, and seafood.

## Watch what you eat!

If you often get a tummy ache after a meal, your body might be sending you a message that a certain food doesn't agree with you. Your doctor can send you for allergy tests to better understand what suits your body.

## Intolerances

A person with an intolerance lacks the enzymes (proteins produced by the body) to digest certain foods. Intolerances are less serious than allergies, as the symptoms are milder: bloating, nausea and diarrhea. Intolerances involving the lactose found in milk, cream and certain cheeses and the gluten in bread and pasta are the most common.

# Waste not, want not

One third of the world's food—in homes, stores and restaurants—ends up in the trash! It's money down the drain and a needless waste of energy. What can we do to reduce waste?

## Plan your purchases

Keep a shopping list to avoid buying items you won't have time to eat and end up having to throw out.

## Organize your pantry

Rotate your food so the stuff that expires first is in front and won't be forgotten!

## Check the expiration date

Before buying an item, look at its expiration date. Ask yourself if you'll have time to eat it before it goes bad. If you find an item in your kitchen that has expired, examine and smell it before throwing it out . . . some expired products are still good to eat!

## Doggy bag!

If you're at a restaurant and can't finish your plate, ask them to wrap it up so you can take it home to eat later.

## Are your eyes bigger than your stomach?

Whether you're at a buffet or a canteen, it's best to go back for seconds than to take too much and not finish it.

# Reduce packaging

Often, the food we eat comes in lots of packaging. Packaging can pollute the environment, when it's being both made and recycled. There are several solutions for reducing waste.

## Bag it!

Why not grab a bag from the house instead of buying one at the store?

## Buy in bulk

Some stores sell food in bulk and allow you to fill your own jars and bags. Pasta, rice, nuts, lentils, and oils are common bulk items.

## Go straight to the source

Buying direct from a farm or market is a good way to avoid packaging.

## Carry a water bottle

Before heading out, grab a reusable water bottle. That way, you don't have to buy a plastic or glass bottle that will end up as garbage.

## What about recycling?

Many types of packaging can be recycled, which is great—such as cardboard, glass and metal—but try to avoid it, if you can, because recycling uses energy, too.

121

# Choose your food

## For your health

Everything you eat stays in your body and can be good or bad for your health! Making good food choices is a way to take care of yourself and stay in shape.

## The choice is yours

When we're little, our parents decide what we eat. But when you grow up, you get to make your own decisions about food.

## For the planet

Your food choices also have an impact on the planet. To protect the environment, you might choose to avoid excessive packaging or buy local products in-season. Lowering your meat consumption is also a good idea because meat production requires a lot of water and contributes to deforestation. Methane gas from cows is also released, greatly contributing to global warming.

**Omnivorous diet**
Omnivorous people eat everything.

**Flexitarian diet**
Those who are flexitarian eat meat, but only occasionally.

**Vegetarian diet**
Vegetarians refuse to eat to animal flesh (meat or fish), but do eat other animal products, such as milk or eggs.

**Vegetalian diet**
Vegetalians consume no animal products whatsoever: no meat, no fish, no honey, no eggs, and no dairy.

**Vegan lifestyle**
Vegans will not consume or buy any product that involves the exploitation of animals: food, leather, fur, and products tested on animals.

Go to **hello.helvetiq.com/ ourbigtable** to download activities to do at school or at home!

Includes Common Core aligned teachers' resources for using *Our Big Table* in the classroom.

**Color some food**

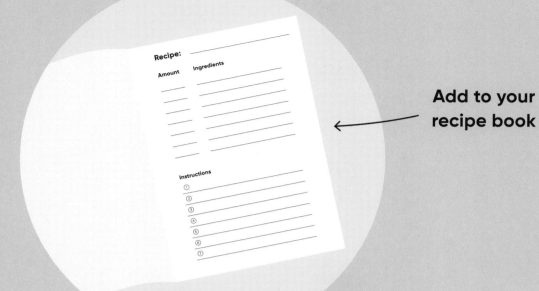

**Add to your recipe book**

**Print a memory card game!**

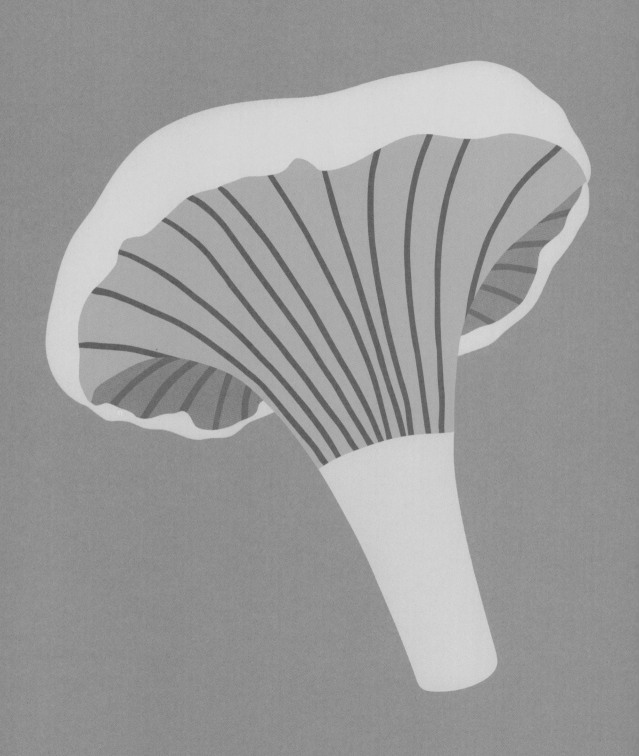

# A word from the author

My name is Lisa Voisard and I was born in Lausanne, Switzerland, in 1992. I am an illustrator, graphic artist and musician. For me, cooking is an opportunity to let my creative juices flow. It's almost meditative! Every spring, I love to eat early-season asparagus; summer is a time to indulge on nectarines; in the fall, a nice squash soup keeps me warm; and a good potato purée goes down well in winter. Sharing a meal with those I love is almost sacred. I'll never forget my nonna's polenta, my father's pizzas, my mother's vegetable pies, my cousins' brownies and curries, my aunt's lasagna . . . My own specialties include peanut butter cookies and fresh pasta.

I'm lactose intolerant and when I was 18, I decided to stop eating meat. So now, most of the time I cook vegan because it's the food choice that suits me best! These dietary restrictions led to my interest in nutrition. I am a firm believer that everyone should get to know their gut and their body. What better way is there to take care of them? Go ahead—taste, experiment and, above all, enjoy!

# Thank you!

To Aude Pidoux, Angela Wade, Hadi Barkat and the entire team at Helvetiq for their incredible editorial and promotional work, and for believing so passionately in my projects.

To Marie Bole-Feysot and Julien Leuenberger from the Department of Botany at the Naturéum in Lausanne, Switzerland, for science-proofing this book, to Jeffrey Butt for the excellent translation, and to Malik Beytrison, Yvan Schneider and Karin Waldhauser for their proofreading skills. To Marie Ganguillet and Isabelle Schwager for their visual input.

To my family and others near and dear to my heart, for supporting me on all my adventures.

To Planet Earth, who provides us with so many beautiful things to see and eat!

# Be Thankful for
# PLANTS

Harriet Ziefert • Brian Fitzgerald

Red Comet Press  Brooklyn

**HARRIET ZIEFERT** has written over two hundred books for children, including the Really Bird series of beginning readers, and *Is a Book a Box for Words?*, for Red Comet Press. She lives and works in the Berkshires, Massachusetts.

**BRIAN FITZGERALD** is an internationally recognized, award-winning illustrator who lives and works in Ireland. The first book that he authored and illustrated, *Bunny's Most Fabulous Vacation Ever!*, was also published by Red Comet Press.

*Be Thankful for Plants*
Text copyright © 2025 Harriet Ziefert
Illustrations copyright © 2025 Brian Fitzgerald
Published in 2025 by Red Comet Press, LLC, Brooklyn, NY

Library of Congress Control Number: 2024939785
ISBN (HB): 978-1-63655-133-3
ISBN (EBOOK): 978-1-63655-134-0
25 26 27 28 29 TLF 10 9 8 7 6 5 4 3 2 1

First Edition
Printed in China

**RED COMET PRESS**
RedCometPress.com

## FIRST

# A plant is animal food.

Would animals be satisfied
without plants?
They would not!

Leaves for gorillas,
Food for antelopes,

Grasses for zebras on African slopes...

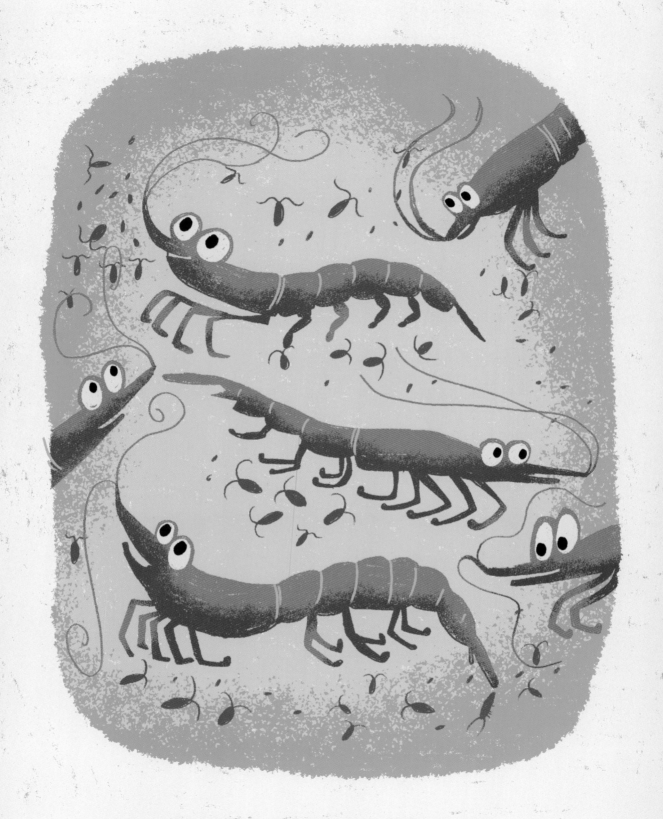

Plankton for small krill,

Greens for manatees...

Plants provide food in big oceans and seas.

Chipmunks munch berries.

Wild lovebirds crunch seeds.

Pollen is food for fuzzy bumblebees.

Elephants and mice,

Big and little beasts...

All think of plants
as the greatest of feasts!

## SECOND

# A plant is people food.

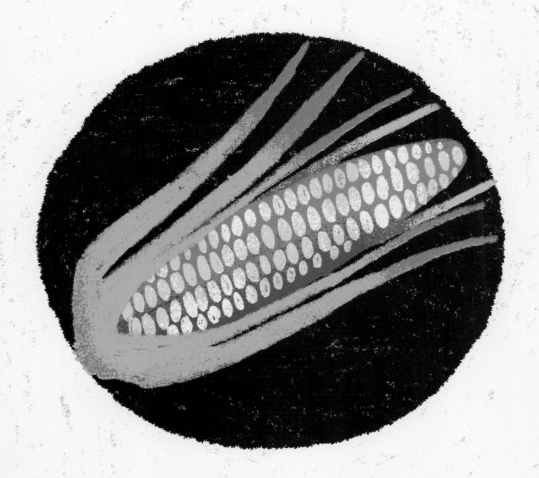

Would people be hungry
without plants?
Yes, they would!

Lettuce for salad,
Fresh fruit for a pie,

Flour to make bread—
hummus on dark rye!

"No," say vegetarians to meat, chicken, fish...

For a plant-based diet is what they wish!

Potatoes, spinach,
cranberries, fresh beans...
Meals are boring without
veggies and greens.

# A plant is shelter.

Would animals and people
stay safe without plants?
They would not!

Robins in bushes,

Butterflies in shrubs,

A badger in weeds with her baby cubs.

A house made of twigs,
Another of sod,

A thatched umbrella is shady and mod.

Newts, salamanders,
Snails, turtles, and snakes...

...make homes in tall grasses
near ponds and near lakes.

Leaves shelter wee snails.

Bushes hide rabbits—
Look, two scared cottontails!

# FOURTH

# A plant is beauty.

Would the world be beautiful
without plants?
It would not!

Flowers in vases,
Two wedding bouquets...

Backyard gardens brighten our days.

Between boulders and rocks,
Plants grow in small spaces.

Plants survive in the harshest of places.

# A plant is comfort.

Would life be comfy
without plants?
It would not!

A mat to sleep on,
A cotton pillow,

Baskets for storage, woven of willow.

Blankies and "lovies" are hugged every day.

Babies and toddlers without them?
No way!

Bedsheets of linen,
Bunk beds of bamboo,

Kid's pajamas made from plant fibers, too.

Sneakers and backpacks,
Hemp shoes and straw caps...

Towels are perfect as cozy beach wraps.

Hoodies, jeans, T-shirts,

Socks, shorts, ties for long hair...

Whatever you wear, plant fibers are there!

## SIXTH

# A plant is protection.

Would life be good
without plants?
It would not!

Grasses guard sand dunes...

...and protect a bird's marsh.

Roots hold dry soil if weather is harsh.

In autumn, leaves fall...

But plants do not die.

They nourish the soil...and fortify!

In desert...

And jungle...

Wetland...

And plain,

Plants are providers—
But need sun and need rain.

## SEVENTH

# A plant is life.

Would life be possible
without plants?
It would not!

Plants keep us healthy—
they freshen the air.

They brighten our day, anytime...anywhere!

Plants are in danger...

...from what people do.

Replacing fields with malls...

...and adding highways, too!

Plants are dying from drought
and from flame.

Pollution and climate change
are to blame.

Plants need protection,
Since plants help us, so...

Let's do what we can
to help plants grow.

Let's give a big cheer,
Sing songs and chant chants,
To Earth's wondrous greenery,

BE THANKFUL FOR PLANTS!